Teaching Through Encouragement

ROBERT J. MARTIN, Ph.D., has worked extensively with in-service professionals in education to increase the effectiveness of teachers, counselors, administrators, and parents. His articles have appeared in *Learning* magazine, *The Humanist Educator*, *The Individual Psychologist*, and other publications. He is a member of the North American Society of Adlerian Psychology, the American Educational Research Association, and the American Personnel and Guidance Association.

Teaching Through Encouragement

Techniques to help students learn

ROBERT J. MARTIN

A SPECTRUM BOOK

PRENTICE-HALL, Inc., Englewood Cliffs, New Jersey 07632

Library of Congress Cataloging in Publication Data

MARTIN, ROBERT J
    Teaching through encouragement.

    (A Spectrum Book)
    Bibliography: p.
    Includes index.
    1. Motivation in education. 2. Students—
Attitudes. 3. Students—Psychology. I. Title.
LB1065.M338   370.15'4   80–15381
ISBN 0-13-896266-9
ISBN 0-13-896258-8 (pbk.)

Editorial/production supervision and
interior design by Suse L. Cioffi
Cover design by Ira Shapiro
Manufacturing buyer: Cathie Lenard

10　9　8　7　6　5　4　3　2

Printed in the United States of America

PRENTICE-HALL INTERNATIONAL, INC., *London*
PRENTICE-HALL OF AUSTRALIA PTY. LIMITED, *Sydney*
PRENTICE-HALL OF CANADA, LTD., *Toronto*
PRENTICE-HALL OF INDIA PRIVATE LIMITED, *New Delhi*
PRENTICE-HALL OF JAPAN, INC., *Tokyo*
PRENTICE-HALL OF SOUTHEAST ASIA PTE. LTD., *Singapore*
WHITEHALL BOOKS LIMITED, *Wellington, New Zealand*

To my colleague, friend and wife, Suzanne Martin, and to the
teachers who encouraged and influenced me:
Herbert Brun
Rudolf Dreikurs
Joan Levy
Paul Painter
Heinz Von Foerster

Contents

Preface

The purpose of this book is to increase the effectiveness of teachers and parents in coping with problems and in encouraging students to cooperate and to learn. It is a personal book: Although the concepts are drawn from humanistic theories of psychology, I have used my own experience and those of teachers I have worked with to speak about the process of encouraging cooperation and responsibility. Rather than telling the reader what to do, the book attempts to help the reader to rethink common experiences and to develop insights from this thinking through. It is not intended as a textbook that provides complete coverage of all available techniques. It is intended to stimulate thinking and to provide suggestions for teachers and parents on interacting more effectively with children.

The key concepts of the book are encouragement and responsibility. Children (and adults) who misbehave, who refuse to cooperate, or who seem too unwilling or too lazy to learn are discouraged human beings who have little sense of their own abilities to change themselves or their world. There may be exceptions to this statement, but they are rare. Children and adults who do not accept responsibility for their own behavior cannot discover their own power to change. In the past, teachers and parents have relied upon reward and punishment, praise and criticism, carrot and stick to induce conformity. These methods no longer work well, for, just as majority groups have lost their power over minority groups (whites over non-whites, men over women), adults have lost their power to control children through coercion. Although these changes create problems, they are a step forward in getting away from authoritarian methods that rob adults and children alike of responsibility and freedom.

Encouragement and responsibility are intertwined. Responsible action is not based on obedience, on law, or even on ethics and morals. Responsible action is based on care and concern for oneself and for others, on a sense of belonging, and on the experience of taking action and living with the consequence of that action.

The book focuses on what teachers can do to change themselves: their ways of understanding events; their attitudes; their ways of handling problems; and, most of all, their ways of communicating. When teachers focus on their own behaviors and on what they can change, they experience a sense of power and encouragement. As long as teachers attempt to control others or their environment, they feel frustrated, angry, resentful, and tired because they are attempting an unending and impossible task. When they concentrate on their behaviors—including feelings and attitudes—they can no longer be easily manipulated, discouraged, or drawn into power struggles. When teachers succeed in encouraging students to accept responsibility for their own behavior, students also experience a sense of power and encouragement that makes mutual cooperation and problem solving possible.

The concepts and techniques that make an approach based on

encouragement and responsibility possible and realistic come from humanistic psychology, especially the work of Rudolf Dreikurs, Carl Rogers, Albert Ellis, and William Glasser.

The basic principles of giving encouragement, of building on strengths, of being a group leader, of avoiding power struggles and special service, and of teaching responsibility are those of my teacher, Rudolf Dreikurs, and his teacher, Alfred Adler. The approach I have used to analyze self-defeating language and beliefs is based on the work of Albert Ellis. The techniques of listening and of using statements with the word "I," techniques so well-known that they can be found in almost any book on counseling, are those of Carl Rogers and of one of his colleagues who has applied Rogers' techniques to teaching, Thomas Gordon. The technique of encouraging students to accept responsibility for their own behavior is based on the work of William Glasser.

The basic idea of examining the strategies children use to cope with school, as well as some of the specific strategies discussed in the book, comes from the work of teacher/author John Holt. The discussion of the fear of failure also owes much to Holt's work. The examples used were provided by teachers and are used with their permission.

Responsibility for the interpretation and development of all techniques and concepts belongs, of course, to the author.

ACKNOWLEDGMENTS

I wish to acknowledge my debt to my teacher, Rudolf Dreikurs, whose thinking permeates this work. I wish to thank my students, especially those who have contributed their experiences to this book. My thanks goes to friends, colleagues, and students who have read portions of the manuscript in its various stages, providing suggestions and encouragement. Special thanks go to Nancy D. Kiger, Ed.D., and John H. Ross, Ed.D., who read the manuscript in its entirety. Finally, my deepest appreciation to Suzanne L. Martin, who read, edited, and evaluated all the various drafts of this book over a five year period.

1
chapter

Encouragement: Basic Principles

Students who act unmotivated, uncooperative, defiant, or irresponsible are discouraged human beings. They feel that they have little or no control over their behavior or their feelings and little or no power to influence their environment. They react defensively by withdrawing, by refusing to cooperate, by giving up, or by seeming to be "lazy," or they react offensively by causing trouble, by fighting, or by talking back.

Encouragement is the process of encouraging: of imparting courage or confidence. The encouragement process is not a way of inducing students to conform through the use of praise or reward but a process of helping students to change their views of self, others, and the world. Let us look at how this can be accomplished.

THE ENCOURAGEMENT PROCESS

Changing Self-Image. Students (and teachers) who feel discouraged typically have a poor self-image. They don't like themselves very much. They feel they're stupid, bad, ugly, or incompetent, and they feel that everyone else must agree with them in their self-evaluations. Students who think poorly of themselves are unlikely to change their attitudes or behavior. Attempting to change people by focusing on their weaknesses seldom works; focusing on weakness reinforces feelings of worthlessness or inferiority. A positive self-image can best be encouraged by focusing on strengths.

Changing Attitudes. Encouragement is a process of helping to change self-defeating attitudes and behavior. Students who have self-defeating attitudes may feel that they can't win, that everyone is unfair, or that no one likes them. As a result, they tend to provoke the behavior that they expect but don't want. A child who expects rejection mistrusts others and questions their motives, inviting rejection. A student who wants to be liked so much that he or she plays the class clown invites others to laugh at him or her rather than accept him or her as a friend. A child who feels that he or she is treated unfairly by adults provokes power struggles in which adults feel forced to punish him or her.

Changing Behavior. Encouragement is a process of helping others to change their behavior. When behavior changes, self-image and attitudes are also likely to change. Conversely, when attitudes and self-image change, behavior is also likely to change.

Encouragement and Responsibility. Encouragement and responsibility are linked. Students who learn to accept responsibility for their behavior experience a sense of power to direct their own lives that gives them the confidence to learn and to cooperate with others. As students begin to change in ways that help them to learn and to cooperate, they feel encouraged by their success.

BUILDING ON STRENGTHS

Our culture encourages us to attempt to "improve" ourselves or others by concentrating on weaknesses. This seldom works because it serves to reinforce feelings of discouragement and hopelessness. Even someone who is talented and successful can be devastated by destructively focusing on a weakness. The following report is by an excellent teacher who recalls her own experience as a college student:

> Sometimes an individual is unable to come up with alternatives to a bad situation — in my case, failure. I had started taking violin lessons when I was five years old. By the time I was ready for college, I was skilled enough to be offered a scholarship to Drake University. But because of my desire to study with a particular teacher, I turned down the scholarship and enrolled at the University of Colorado. My first year was very rewarding. I worked very hard, but the recognition I received and the opportunities to perform far outweighed the work factor.
>
> During the last semester of my sophomore year, I enrolled in a required course called Solfeggio — a sort of glorified ear training and dictation class. I had never had any training along these lines, and I was almost out of my mind with fear and worry. Even with a tutor, the course was impossible for me. Toward the end of the semester, the Solfeggio professor called me to his office, but instead of telling me to keep working as he had in the past, he informed me that I was failing the course and that it would be impossible for me to succeed in counterpoint, orchestration, or composition knowing as little as I did about Solfeggio. He suggested I drop out of Music School. So I did. When you wrote that failure reduces a person to the level of a frightened animal, I agree.

The teacher who wrote this was not, by the way, a music teacher. Despite all of her strengths in the area of music, she was overwhelmed by the experience.

You can only build on strengths. No matter how weak, inadequate, handicapped, or discouraged they may be, individuals can only be helped by finding and building on areas of strength — areas where the individuals are capable of helping themselves.

Look for Strengths. Particularly with difficult students, it is easy to see only the negative side, only the problems. We are aware of deficits and problems because they make life difficult for us. It may be necessary to take a few minutes and to think of a student's strengths.

The more students seem unable to help themselves, the more necessary it becomes to focus on strengths and to avoid unnecessary dependence. The following example was provided by an observer in an orthopedically handicapped class:

> Two of the children who were the most severely handicapped could do nothing for themselves when they entered the class. As a result of being in the class, one of the children learned to wheel himself to the bathroom in two minutes when it had previously taken him twenty-two minutes. One of the things the other child learned to do was take off and put on her coat. One day when the bus was waiting to take the students home, the teacher started putting the little girl's coat on for her because they were running behind schedule. The little boy said, "What in the world are you doing? Don't you think she can do that herself?"

The teacher already knew that the girl could put her coat on, but she didn't realize what she was doing until one of the other students pointed out that the teacher was taking over in the area of the girl's strengths. The child's self-concept and the educational gains that had been made with this child were more important than the bus having to wait an extra few minutes. The teacher did not feel defensive about the incident but was pleased that her students were becoming more independent:

> The teacher said that the feeling she got from the experience was unbelievable. She said it only takes a few of those experiences to

keep her going strong and make her feel that she is accomplishing her task.

Take Students Seriously. The basis of encouraging others is to take them seriously. There is no substitute for sincere interest. Without a willingness to become involved with students as human beings, the practices suggested in books and articles on effective teaching become empty exercises.

We know what it means to be taken seriously from our own experiences. We have all had experiences where we felt someone was listening, expressing interest, and even agreeing without caring in the least. When asked for an opinion that is then ignored, we feel frustrated. When administrators ask for committee reports and recommendations only to give their school an appearance of democracy, teachers feel cheated and resentful. In the same way, students also feel discouraged, frustrated, and resentful when teachers appear to listen and take an interest but really don't care.

Take an Interest. Taking an interest in what students are thinking and doing is often a much more powerful form of encouragement than praise.

- Take time to listen and observe.
- Re-structure class time when necessary so that you do have time to listen and observe. A teacher who spends most of the time lecturing or correcting papers or worksheets doesn't have time to just watch. Observing students may seem to some teachers like sitting and doing nothing, but often more can be learned by simply watching students than can be learned from hours of testing.
- When you're taking others seriously, you're trying to learn as well as teach. Find out what students think and what their attitudes are. Even if you know more than they do about something they're interested in, be careful about giving help until help is wanted.

Build On a Student Interest. In the following example, a special education teacher shares an example of building on a student's attention to the "wrong" thing:

> Billy, who is in my EMR class and is eight years old, has had difficulty paying attention during a lesson or activity. One day during reading I noticed Billy had a few cars out on his desk and was playing with them. Instead of reprimanding him for not paying attention, I asked Billy to share what he knew about these cars. From what he said and from what other children contributed, we wrote a language-experience story. The children really enjoyed this! After that, when the children had something they wanted to share I encouraged them. Billy has participated more in class lessons and activities since then. I used a problem of inattention as an opportunity for encouragement. This also encouraged the class to be responsible for creating their own learning experiences.

It might seem to some teachers that although Billy was encouraged, the teacher had been diverted from her lesson, and that this could be a problem. Teachers are sometimes unsure about when it is worthwhile to change a lesson and deal with something that comes up on the spur of the moment. In this case, even though the teacher did change what she was doing, she used the student's interest to meet the goals of the lesson.

Many times, teachers make a lesson or an activity an end in itself and then feel threatened when anyone or anything upsets the planned lesson. There are many ways in which a teacher can change a lesson in order to build on the interests and strengths of the students without changing the essence of what he or she is trying to do. As a parent, I feel frustrated when my own children describe incidents where their interests, creativity, and motivation were squelched, not because they had a "bad" teacher but because they had a teacher who was trying so hard to be a good teacher.

The topic that comes up most often in my graduate classes, after the topic of problem behavior, is motivation: How can I motivate students? How can I make students want to learn what they're supposed to? The teacher in the above example didn't try to motivate Billy to pay attention to what she was doing; instead, she decided to pay attention to what *he* was paying attention to.

Inattention Is a Form of Attention. Teachers often say, "You aren't paying attention," but the students *are* paying attention. Inattention is really a way of saying that a student is paying attention to something the teacher isn't interested in. A student who never pays attention is paying attention to something. In the example above, Billy was paying attention to his cars, and the teacher used this as a way of encouraging his participation.

Ask for Help. Don't be self-sufficient. Involve students in decisions and tasks so that they have a contribution to make. Few things are as encouraging as being part of a group where your contribution is needed and appreciated.

Put Success within Reach. Easy success, excessive praise, and over-emphasis on being successful can create more problems than they solve. Yet the experience of success — of reaching a goal, no matter how small, or of completing a task, no matter how simple — is essential to encouragement. Here is an example of such encouragement by a sixth-grade teacher:

> Johnny was a slow learner in my sixth-grade class. He was reading at the third-grade level at the beginning of the year. In our other subjects besides reading, we sometimes read aloud. Johnny was one who never volunteered. Everyone in the class was given a chance to read. At first, in order for him to feel some success, I would try to pick a paragraph that I felt he could read with little difficulty. By the end of the quarter, I could see a definite improvement in his reading ability. He would try harder reading material and would volunteer quite frequently. I even used him as the advanced reader in a group of two readers, which really built up his confidence when he found he could help another person read. By the end of the year, he had progressed almost two years. As a result of this, his work in other subjects improved. What an accomplishment!

Teachers sometimes ask how they can be successful with slower students when they just don't have the time to spend. What made the difference in this example was not the extra time spent by the teacher, but her sensitivity in building Johnny's confidence to challenge himself.

Building on strengths is not simply a matter of encouraging improved academic performance. Students who are discouraged often have a very poor self-image as well as an intense dislike of school. The following example was supplied by an eighth-grade math teacher:

> Doug was placed in my program because of his low grades and poor attendance. I found that Doug had some math skills. I attempted to provide opportunities for success based on his strengths. The work was not on the eighth-grade level, but it was something that provided a meaningful opportunity for success.
>
> Doug was fairly competent with his multiplication facts through the twelve tables. I attempted to place him in situations where he could demonstrate his skills. When he completed an assignment early, I would check it over, discuss the concept with him, and then let him help the other students. When we played games such as "Around the World," Doug moved from a reluctant participant to a skillful champion. In all the activities, Doug knew he had a chance to succeed. He didn't always succeed, but he saw the opportunity for success. He wasn't looking for simple work he had already mastered, and he did not want work that would defeat him before he started. He was looking for an environment in which he could build and develop the skills he had. He needed to feel good about himself. After working with low-level students, I have discovered that most of them want a chance to do their work without the preconceived idea of failure.

Success is important, but this success cannot be artificially provided by the teacher. The teacher who provided the above example writes about his own role in encouraging students:

> I cannot make anyone feel successful for any length of time. I might

be able to help someone feel better about him- or herself but the true feeling of success is perceived by the person who experiences success. Everyone knows when he or she is doing something that is meaningful. This is why teachers cannot manufacture success for their students.

Initially, students may accept the teacher's version of success, but it won't last long. By selling success, the teacher does two things. First, when the facade wears off, students can see that they accomplished nothing. This reinforces the idea that they are not really successful. Second, a phony success destroys the teacher's credibility. In my estimation, when credibility goes, so should the teacher.

Success is not a magic ingredient that can be supplied by teachers. Building on strengths allows students to create their own success, but *when* this success may occur cannot always be predicted. The teacher who wrote the above paragraphs is very much against what he calls "a phony success." One senses in his writing a sincerity and honesty that has nothing to do with manipulating students into doing well. Doug, the boy he describes in his example, did change as a result of his successful experience:

When Doug experienced success, his attitude changed. He seemed happy, and his attendance improved. The success in math carried over to his other subjects, and by the end of the year, Doug's grades were much improved. I think a little success gave him the incentive.

Look for Mistakes that Make Sense. Mistakes are often the result of a logical, though incorrect, approach to solving a problem. Teachers who do not realize when a mistake makes sense are likely to discourage students from thinking.

There are two approaches that teachers can take to a student's answer. The first is characterized by the Frenchman, Binet, who originated what has come to be called the IQ test. Children are asked questions, and their answers are scored as either right or wrong. The second approach is characterized by the Swiss pioneer in the cognitive development of the child, Jean Piaget. Piaget worked with Binet at one time, but he quickly became more interested in *why* a child answered as he or she did rather than what he or she gave as an answer.

The following example took place in a high-school foreign language class:

> Wayne was doing poorly in his Spanish class. When the teacher gave a dictation test, Wayne failed. Very few words were spelled correctly, and the separation between words was not correct. The teacher noticed, however, that Wayne had heard and recorded all of the sounds. She wrote him a note on the test explaining that although he had failed the test, he had picked out the sounds and that if he could learn to group the sounds correctly and learn to spell them, he could do quite well. Wayne began to pay more attention in class, and his work did improve.

The teacher recognized that Wayne's answers did make sense and that he was listening carefully. Although he did not pass the test, apparently he felt encouraged by the teacher's remarks.

THE PROBLEM OF BEING SPECIAL

A commonly held idea about encouragement is that encouraging children to feel special will enhance self-image, cooperation, and performance. Unfortunately, in an effort to be encouraging, teachers and parents sometimes teach a child that he or she is an exception who is entitled to special treatment and consideration. It is essential to distinguish between respecting each individual in his or her uniqueness and encouraging a sense of being a special case.

There are two ways of being special: first, being special in the sense of being a unique individual; and, second, being special in the sense of getting privileged treatment. The second is often confused with the first, and this confusion often leads to problems. Although each of us is unique—a quality to be respected and cherished—this does not mean that the universe should or will make special rules or special exceptions for us. Encouraging a feeling of specialness, in the sense of getting special treatment, is wrongly assumed to encourage a feeling of self-worth and a striving for excellence. The opposite is true: feelings of self-worth and a striving for excellence come from within; these qualities come from the courage to cope with problems and difficulties without having to rely on special treatment. In the following example, a teacher describes the hazards of being special:

> Scott's father was manager of the town's tennis court. He was teaching both his sons how to play, and when I received Scott in second grade he was a very accomplished student of tennis. He knew that he was very accomplished, and he let the rest of the class know that he could beat any of them. Whenever talk of sports came up, Scott would make remarks about tennis. At conference time, any comments I made were put in terms of tennis by his father — such as how you cannot improve your serve without practice, and that you have to do the same for your math facts. Any students who stayed over at his house always went to play tennis, and then Scott would be sure to tell us how he beat his friend.

> As much confidence as he seemed to have, you would think Scott could handle anything. Just the opposite. As the year progressed, Scott alienated many of the other boys. He was so determined to win and be number one that he made up reasons why his team didn't win. He began crying if he wasn't picked to answer questions, and he complained that things weren't fair. He also started blurting out in class instead of waiting to be called on.

In their attempts to encourage Scott to play tennis well, his parents inadvertently made it difficult for Scott to handle situations where he couldn't win. When parents and teachers encourage children to be special, the children may learn to dislike situations where they can't be special.

Acceptable but Mistaken Ways of Being Special

Students who achieve specialness through useful or socially acceptable means are not always recognized as having a problem.

Being good, being charming, getting good grades, and being a winner are usually encouraged in children. Children who find their places in school or in the family mainly through these means can become a problem, however. It's fine to do well, to win a game, to score high on a test, or to be recognized for an accomplishment, but feeling compelled to do these things can be a terrible burden.

It's easy to encourage children in these mistaken goals because our culture encourages us to do so. As in the case of Scott, the child tennis player just discussed, it's also easy to create a demanding, successful, selfish, perhaps even charming monster we can't seem to understand. Every teacher has had students who were a problem because of behavior that once seemed extremely positive to parents and teachers. Sometimes it is difficult to avoid feeling prejudice against these students. A fourth-grade teacher I know had a difficult time sorting out her emotions in dealing with a boy who came from a seemingly advantaged home yet who refused to cooperate unless everything suited him. She found it difficult not to feel angry and frustrated with this poor little rich boy because she felt that he shouldn't have been the way he was. She could understand and be patient with a child from a disadvantaged background, but she had trouble doing so with this child. Yet, in his own way, he was doing his best to live out a role he had learned to play. However mistaken his way of making a place for himself at home and in school, he was doing his best to survive in the only way he knew how. This boy's way of being special was largely negative — refusing to do his work. There are many children whose behavior is exemplary but who secretly feel like ugly ducklings. Unable to meet the standards they think will win them a place in their family, in school, or with their peers, they are unhappy playing the role of the good student, the charmer, the winner, the child prodigy.

Being Good. Children who are good as a means of finding a place in the group or as a means of solving their problems may have difficulty taking initiative, exploring new ideas or experiences, taking risks, or being creative. We need to get away from the concept of teaching children to "be good" and instead to put the emphasis on both cooperation and independence. Many children have felt like this at one time or another:

> I remember being good because I was afraid not to be. I was afraid of getting into trouble, yes, but I was more afraid of losing my reputation as a good child and a good student. I remember in fourth grade being lectured by the teacher. I must not have worked very hard during that term, because my grades were low. I really wasn't even aware of the situation (the grade cards hadn't been handed out yet) until the teacher called me up to her desk and told me how I "was wasting my talents," that I wasn't trying, and whatever else she could to make me feel guilty.

> The lecture must have taken, because I was always careful to get good grades — not just in fourth grade either, but all through school. Yet I can't help thinking that there would have been a better way to handle the situation. I became more compulsive about doing the right thing, but I also became more inhibited about thinking and taking risks, and more compulsive about doing exactly what the teacher wanted.

"Being good" is a role. In addition to being inappropriate in many situations, being good can inhibit a child's ability to act responsibly. Don't encourage being good. When you deal with a child who is overly concerned with being good, be patient and understanding. The child is trying hard to live up to the expectations of adults. Criticism will only generate confusion and resentment.

Using Charm. Charm can be delightful, but it can be a handicap when used as a means of solving problems. When charm becomes a substitute for competence, it interferes with development.

> She was tiny, even for kindergarten, and seemed almost like a doll to the other children. The other children would mother her and try to help her. Perhaps they felt that they were big when they could help someone who was smaller. The little girl would smile and soak up

the attention, but her teacher was concerned that she was becoming dependent on the help and attention that were so lovingly offered.

Special service does not always come from adults, as this example shows.

Recognition. Encouraging students to participate in activities that earn them special recognition can become a problem when students feel that activities that do not earn special recognition are no longer worthwhile. Parents who encourage their children to do special projects may inadvertently discourage them from doing ordinary tasks. Neither should children be discouraged from doing special projects that bring recognition. A problem is likely to result when parents or teachers show an interest in and give recognition only for special projects and not for the ordinary everyday tasks that need to be done.

Helping. Probably every teacher has experienced students who are so overly helpful that they create a problem. In many cases, these children are trying hard to find a place in the class. They want to be liked and accepted. They have decided that being helpful is a way that they can be special. Once we recognize the purpose of the child's behavior, it is much easier to decline an offer of help without putting the child down or without becoming frustrated or angry.

Being a Good Student. Getting good grades, knowing the right answer, and being the teacher's pet: these can be ways of being special, either at school or at home. When these things become ends in themselves, real learning suffers. I want my children to get good grades, but I hope I show at least as much interest in what they're learning as I do in the grade they get; otherwise, they may decide that what they learn isn't important. It's a common complaint that students are much more interested in their grades than in what they've learned, but they've learned from their parents and teachers to be interested in the grades. The recognition given to high grades and right answers teaches children that these things are more important than what they learn.

Being Special and Special Service

Don't encourage feelings of being special by providing special service that students don't need. If teachers politely ignore or refuse demands for special service, students will quickly adjust.

The feeling of being special leads easily to demands for special service. Students who believe that they are special will expect and demand special service. A friend who was a dean of students at a small private college said that most of the students who came to see him believed that they were special cases and that exceptions should be made for them. They had been given special treatment in the past, and they expected it to continue in college. The next chapter examines the problem of special service and considers how teachers can help without providing such service.

SUMMARY

Encouragement is the process of helping students to change the ways in which they think, feel, and act, so that they can accept, and exercise responsibility for their own behavior. Focusing on weaknesses only discourages students.

Trying to make students feel special may seem like a positive approach, but it often leads to mistaken ideas of being superior or of being an exception. Students can best be encouraged by focusing on strengths rather than on weaknesses.

2
chapter

Special Service*

One of the myths of teaching is that teachers should always be helpers. Teachers are encouraged to think that helping others is always desirable and that it's the teacher's job to help wherever and whenever possible. Yet determination to help students can encourage dependent and irresponsible behavior. We have all experienced the feeling of trying to help and of finding out help isn't wanted or that we're being taken advantage of. When this happens, we feel anger, resentment, and hurt.

*The concept of special service is based on the work of Rudolf Dreikurs, M.D.; see discussions of attention getting in Rudolf Dreikurs, *Psychology in the Classroom*, 1968. Also see Rudolf Dreikurs, B. Grunwald and F. Pepper, *Maintaining Sanity in the Classroom*, 1971.

Following unexamined impulses to help can lead to smothering, dominating care on the one hand or to indifference on the other. The key to avoiding both of these undesirable alternatives is to understand how to give help without providing special service.

Special service is anything you do for students that they would be better off doing for themselves. This definition is obviously a subjective one—as it has to be; *you* must decide what is special service and what isn't.

DEALING WITH DEMANDS FOR SPECIAL SERVICE

Busy teachers often fail to see that they are providing a great deal of unnecessary help. The most difficult part of coping with demands for special service is recognizing the problem:

> Paul was a student in a beginning Bench Wood Laboratory who had taxed the teacher's patience because of his inability to understand directions. One day the students were busy planing boards. Paul was having trouble, so the teacher went over to him. Paul looked up, his eyes flaring, and said that the plane wasn't cutting correctly. The teacher asked Paul if he had set the plane correctly, and he replied that he had. The teacher looked at the plane, readjusted it, and started planing Paul's board. Paul smiled, and the teacher left his bench. About ten minutes later, Paul came up to the teacher and insisted that his plane wasn't working correctly. The teacher returned to Paul's bench and adjusted the plane. Ten minutes later, Paul came to the teacher again with the same problem. This time, the teacher realized what was going on and told Paul that he would explain how to set the plane one more time and that Paul would then have to take care of it himself. Since that time Paul never asked the teacher to do something without trying to do it first himself.

The teacher solved the problem easily enough once he recognized the problem. The surprising thing is that this scene took place in a college class rather than in a high school class. The teacher commented, "I didn't think students would use these strategies past elementary and high school." The real lesson in this example, however, was revealed to the teacher later when he was counseling Paul about his lack of confidence. Paul agreed that he lacked confidence and added that ever sincé he could remember, his father had been afraid that Paul would hurt himself or had insisted that he could do the job better than Paul anyway. Unwillingness to try was a result of long-standing discouragement.

Avoid Repeating Questions, Answers, and Directions. The only way out of this is to tell students that you'll say what you have to say once and that you will not repeat it. And then don't repeat it. It's amazing how easily we can be trapped into repeating:

> The teacher was a graduate student teaching a class of college freshmen. Because she wanted everyone to do well, she would repeat directions several times for the slower students. This was causing a problem with discipline and morale because the rest of the class was getting bored. After sharing her problem with a group of other teachers, she became aware that in her efforts to be a good teacher she was rewarding the students who didn't pay attention and discouraging those who listened. She was afraid of losing some students by telling her class that she would give directions only once, but she agreed to try it. She was surprised and pleased to find that although some of the poor students did not do better, others were listening more closely and that the overall attitude of the class had improved.

When a teacher feels compelled to give special service, those who are getting the special service may end up controlling what happens in class, as can be seen in this example.

Ignore Demands for Attention. Not all demands for attention are legitimate. Teachers have no obligation to respond automatically to all demands for attention.

> Ed, a third-grade student, was constantly at the teacher's desk asking unnecessary questions in order to get attention. Her response was to explain that she did not have time but that she would look at his

work later. This didn't discourage Ed, and he would be back ten
minutes later, asking for help or wanting special attention.

When the teacher described in this example brought up the
problem in my graduate class of in-service teachers, she couldn't
understand why Ed continued to bother her when she was trying
so hard to discourage him. At first, she was inclined to blame the
boy's parents and home life, saying that he often dominated things
at home. She was surprised when the class discussed how her behavior was reinforcing Ed. In her attempts to discourage him from
coming up to the desk, she was giving him the attention he was
looking for.

Some teachers might wonder, as I did, why it was necessary
for the teacher to be at her desk in the first place instead of moving around the room working with individual students or groups.
Nevertheless, the real problem was that the teacher was reinforcing
Ed's behavior. She may have been correct that Ed used this strategy, as well as others, to dominate his family and that he was trying out the same strategy with her, but she didn't understand that
she was cooperating with his behavior. She had originally said
that she was ignoring him, and she at first found it difficult to ac-
ept that talking to Ed — no matter what she was saying — was not
ignoring him. When asked if she would be willing to ignore Ed by
not talking to him or even looking at him when he came to her
desk, she wasn't sure that she could do it. Her image of a good
teacher didn't allow her to ignore Ed — even though her behavior
was only making his behavior worse. We had to talk her into it,
and she still wasn't convinced that she could ignore him. I was
skeptical about any change coming, not because the teacher was
not cooperative but because her ideas about being a good teacher
were so strong. I was surprised the next week when she reported
that she had kept quiet and that it had worked. Ed had been much
improved, and she had also found times during the day when she
could give him positive attention rather than the negative attention she had been giving him.

Students may demand attention they don't need because they

are so anxious to do well. In the following example, a sixth-grade teacher describes a student who creates a problem when he attempts to follow his mother's advice:

> Help! I have a student who asks me a question on practically every problem in math class. He always wants to be assured that he is working the problems correctly. During the parent conference, I mentioned the problem to his mother. She said that she had told him that he could get good grades if he asked plenty of questions.

This student wants to do well and please his parents. He is capable of doing the problems, but seems to lack confidence in himself:

> When he asks me about each problem, I always ask him to tell me the steps to working the problem. Then I tell him to work through the problem using those steps, and he usually comes up with the right answer without me actually working the problem. However, he always feels that it is necessary to find out if he has worked each problem correctly immediately after he works it. I hope he will see that he is capable of doing his math without relying on the teacher so much.

The teacher sees and understands the problem quite clearly. What he doesn't see is that although he didn't create the problem, he is continuing to reinforce the boy's behavior by continuing to provide the special service. The student needs to be given a chance to find out that he can do the problems on his own, and the only way to do this is to withdraw the special attention he is getting. As it is, the special help seems to be reinforcing the student's feeling that he can't do the work by himself. The teacher is already aware of a possible solution and needs only to implement it:

> I find it tempting to tell him to sit down, work the problems by himself, and turn them in to see how many he can get right on his own. I'm sure he can do quite well.

This student is more likely to be encouraged by withdrawing the special service than by continuing it.

Don't Do for Others What They Can Do for Themselves. We need to be willing to find out what children can do by giving them a chance to do things on their own. Too often, adults don't know what children can do because they don't give the children a chance.

The following example was shared by a teacher's aide in a special education class.

Sally was an eighteen-year-old mentally retarded student in a special education class. She seldom finished eating lunch on schedule, which created a problem for the next class, since her class waited until she was finished before leaving. The teacher couldn't understand why the girl didn't do better, since the teacher constantly reminded her to finish. Perhaps she felt that Sally, being mentally retarded, couldn't do any better.

Sally's teacher agreed to tell Sally that she would have till the end of the period to finish her dinner and that if she wasn't finished, that was O.K., but that she would have to leave at that time. The teacher let her know when she had five minutes left, and, to the teacher's surprise, Sally finished without any problems.

It was only by allowing Sally to be responsible for her own behavior that the teacher and Sally found out that she could finish on time.

HELPING WITHOUT GIVING
SPECIAL SERVICE

The following suggestions are intended not as rules but as guidelines for examining helping relationships. Although the focus here is on adult–child relationships, these guidelines apply to all helping relationships.

Decide What You're Willing to Do. It's extremely difficult not to feel resentful when you do things for others that you really don't want to do. This resentment is bound to come out in one way or another and, in turn, to generate resentment and guilt feelings in the person you're trying to help.

Don't confuse not liking something with not being willing to do it. There are many things we don't particularly like doing that we're willing to do. Willingness means accepting responsibility for what we do. When parents or teachers make sacrifices for children because they feel they have to, they aren't accepting responsibility for their decision: they're blaming circumstances—or even the children—for having to make the sacrifices. Children who receive help under these conditions are often made to feel guilty. Naturally they don't feel grateful, and they might prefer to do without the help.

When you set limits based on what you're willing to do, your relationships with students are likely to improve because your students will know that when you give help you give it willingly. Sometimes we find it difficult to set limits because we want to be liked, to be accepted. The absence of limits, however, creates uneasiness and mistrust. If you are honest with yourself and others about what you're willing to do—and if you then stick to what you say—you will still be accepted.

One example of a problem where teachers sometimes get trapped into doing something they are not willing to do is the matter of providing pencils, pens, books, paper, and so on to students who forget them. Junior high and high school teachers find this more of a problem than elementary teachers because they have more students in the course of a day. The problem seems like a trivial one, but in every group of teachers I have worked with there are at least a few who find themselves really frustrated and upset when students do forget. They feel that they are responsible, and yet they don't know what to do.

One way for teachers to cope with their own anger and frustration about forgotten items is to put the responsibility for the problem back on the student. Different teachers have different methods of doing this. With pens and pencils, for example, some teachers keep a box of pens or pencils they sell to students; others "rent out" pencils for a fee or require a deposit to make sure that they get their pencils back; still other teachers tell students that they'll have to figure something out and that it's their problem. By finding a solution that puts the problem and the responsibility back on the student, the teacher can handle the situation without becoming angry and without putting down the students or nagging them. Decide how much and what kind of help you're willing to give, and then let the student know where you stand. Giving help can be made part of a contract between the people involved: I'm willing to do such-and-such if you're willing to do such-and-such. Teachers and students don't need to feel that help is a one-way street with the teacher on the giving end. Students who want help need to be willing to cooperate by accepting the terms of the help and by doing their part.

Make a Compromise Where Possible. Avoiding special service does not mean leaving students on their own. Students need encouragement, not special service. The following example was provided by an elementary teacher who found a way to encourage a student in a difficult situation by making a compromise:

> A girl came to me after every problem she worked to ask if she had done it correctly. She was a very smart little girl and almost always had the correct answer. Her constant questions almost drove me crazy. Finally I talked with her and told her it bothered me because she was such a smart little girl and could do it alone. We compromised, and I looked over her work when all of it was done. She was still getting positive reinforcement and was no longer driving me crazy.

The teacher seems to have handled this situation well. She might have avoided the "because you are such a smart girl" routine. Using logic of this type often causes resentment. As this example shows, however, handling a situation in an "ideal way" is not always necessary in order to achieve a satisfactory result.

Avoid Giving Solutions. Helping others can easily become an attempt to solve their problems for them. Good counseling consists in helping others to help themselves.

If you give a solution, then you're likely to be held responsible for its working or not working. You wouldn't tell a friend whether or not to get a divorce because that decision must be made by the friend. What makes a solution viable is that it is a decision. If you suggest a solution, the solution may be a good one, but the child will not have made a decision to carry out that solution. The child will feel that you're responsible for carrying out the solution. Even if the child agrees to go along with the solution, this is not the same as making a commitment to carrying out that solution.

Don't Pretend to Know More Than You Do. You don't have to answer every question or have a solution for every problem. You'll have more credibility and you'll be teaching children to have a realistic picture of things if you don't try to live up to an impossible image.

Avoid playing expert. It's nice to be treated as an expert, but you can get caught in the trap of trying to solve a problem that you can't or shouldn't have tried to solve.

Encourage a Sense of Control. Students who cannot cope with problems or who misbehave often have no sense of being able to control their own actions. Children—and adults—learn to act responsibly only when they are convinced that their actions have consequences and that they have the power to act differently and thus change those consequences in the future.

It sometimes seems that students have too much power, but students who successfully manipulate teachers are often unaware of the power they have to make situations worse—or better.

The goal of encouragement is to increase an individual's sense of being able to change what happens by changing his or her own behavior. Help is encouraging when it results in a greater feeling of responsibility and independence on the part of the person helped rather than in a greater feeling of being dependent and powerless.

Children who feel that they are failures are often convinced that that's the way they are and that there's nothing they can do about it. Students who are labeled as troublemakers often feel that they are just "bad" and that that's the way they are.

CHANGING MYTHS ABOUT
SPECIAL SERVICE

Teachers and parents who want to stop giving special service sometimes feel torn. They want to be effective, but they also want to live up to the image they have of the "good teacher" or the "good parent." The thought of cutting off special service often brings with it a flood of rationalizations in defense of continuing special service. Most of these rationalizations are myths we have been taught, and we easily feel guilty if we ignore them. We judge ourselves by the norms we've grown up with. Even when we're convinced intellectually that these norms are no longer valid, we find it difficult not to feel uneasy and guilty when we ignore them.

When we're using our energy trying to be good teachers, we easily become more concerned about our images and what we're doing than we are about what the students are learning and how we can help them. The same problem comes with parenting. When we're concerned with being good parents, we're often more concerned with how the neighbors, the children's teacher, a visitor, or a mother-in-law will judge us as parents than we are about helping or enjoying children.

We maintain the myth of the goodness of providing special service by what we tell ourselves. The following statements about special service *sound* true because we have heard them so often without really examining them:

It's My Responsibility. It's not the teacher's job to provide special service. It is the teacher's responsibility to decide whether or not special service would really help the student to learn and develop. Teachers (and parents) are encouraged to feel overly responsible for those entrusted to them. As a result, teachers inadvertently

train students to act in irresponsible ways. Even teachers who
want to encourage independence may find themselves feeling
angry, guilty, or anxious when students come to them with a problem. At such times, teachers might, if they were to observe themselves, find that they feel responsible and that they tell themselves
one or several of the following:

- I *should* be able to do something.
- Why do they come to me with this? What can I do?
- If only they had listened or had had more sense, this
  wouldn't have happened.
- I'm going to get blamed if this doesn't get straightened
  out.
- If only I knew what to do.
- I know exactly what to do.
- I *must* figure out something.
- I *have to do* something!

These sentences and the feelings of resentment (that we're expected to do something we can't do), anger (our advice isn't being
taken), or guilt (we *should* be able to solve every problem) are
learned responses. We are all unique individuals, yet we learn certain standardized ways of responding.

But I Have To Help—It's My Job. You don't always have to help.
A teacher's (parent's) job is not to be a servant who provides help
whether or not it's really needed. The job is to help students to
learn and develop, and this is sometimes done most effectively by
standing back and letting students struggle with a problem instead
of jumping in and helping. It's not your job to solve problems that
belong to students but rather to help students to solve their own
problems.

A Good Teacher Would. . . . Giving special service does not make teachers effective. A teacher who doesn't provide special service may be judged negatively by some parents and teachers who don't realize that special service isn't really helping the child. What makes a professional is not the willingness to rush in and help everyone but the willingness to evaluate and make decisions about what the children need.

Parents and Administrators Expect Me To. . . . Some administrators may not understand why you're doing something. Be prepared to explain why your actions are professional and appropriate to the needs of the children. Even in those cases where an administrator doesn't agree, keep in mind that most administrators are content to let teachers do their job provided it doesn't cause them too many problems.

If I Don't Help, I Don't Care. The opposite is often true. A teacher or parent may want to tell a child what to do and yet refrain from doing so because of concern for the child.

I'll Think Poorly of Myself if I Don't Help. Strong personal involvement in finding a solution to a problem narrows our vision and makes us more likely to make a poor decision. A helper who has a strong personal stake in the outcome of a problem is likely to pay more attention to his or her own need than to the needs of the person with the problem. The irrational decision that we must think less of ourselves if we don't live up to impossible standards of solving everyone's problems actually leads us to interfere in situations where we would be better off not interfering.

I'll Feel Bad if I Don't. Teachers and parents who have been indoctrinated to believe that good teachers and good parents always lend a helping hand will easily feel bad when they try to stand back and let children cope with their own problems. This doesn't mean that teachers and parents *should* feel bad or that they will continue to feel bad if they stop providing unncessary service. Once they see the positive results of avoiding special service, they are more likely to stop feeling guilty.

MAKING EXCEPTIONS

One student wants to turn in an assignment late; another wants to do extra work; another can't study for an exam because of a part-time job; still another was sick and wants to make up an exam. Teachers are constantly being asked to make exceptions.

Making exceptions might seem to be a form of special service, but when making an exception encourages children to become competent and responsible, it's not special service. The argument of avoiding special service can be a way to avoid responsibility. Just as the individual needs of some students require that the teacher avoid giving special service, so the needs of other students may require making an exception. Such exceptions may seem like special service, but remember that special service means doing for others what they can do for themselves.

In my own teaching and parenting I make exceptions fairly often, and, to be honest, I'm not always sure I'm not being conned. When I think I'm encouraging students, I may only be giving special service. On the other hand, if I don't think making an exception would be genuinely encouraging, I am not usually going to be manipulated into making it.

Knowing what is special service and what is a legitimate exception is a creative process that calls for careful observation, decision making, and trial and error. No set rules can replace the teacher's creativity. Teachers are sometimes kept from exercising this creativity, however, by a number of myths.

Myth #1: Teachers Should Be Consistent. Being consistent is often desirable, but not always. Being consistent is not an end in itself. You can decide to handle a problem one way one week and another way another week. Each may be appropriate at the time.

Myth #2: If I Do It for One, I Have to Do It for Everybody. Why do teachers have to do for everybody what they do for one student? The only rational answer is that they don't. There are times when the teacher's life is much easier if the teacher does treat everyone the same, but there is no reason why the teacher has to.

Teachers sometimes feel trapped by students who use logic on them. A student says, "Well you did such-and-such for Susan, so you should do such-and-such for me." The two situations may not even be the same, but the teacher feels manipulated into going along with the student. What has happened is that the teacher feels that he or she has to be consistent, even though he or she knows that the one exception was legitimate and that the present request is not. Or even worse, a teacher makes an exception, realizes later that it was a mistake to do so, yet feels compelled to go along with the student who says, "But you did it before."

Once the teacher realizes that he or she is free to change, telling the student the truth is a simple matter. For example, a teacher might say, "Well, you're right, I did make an exception before, but I realize that was a mistake, and I'm not willing to make an exception now." Or, in a different circumstance: "The circumstances are different, so I don't feel bound by what I did six months ago." The students may not like it, but they will adjust.

Myth #3: I Have to Be Fair. This is just a variant of myths #1 and #2. First, no matter how hard you try, you can't be perfectly fair. It's impossible. The ironic thing, however, is that people who try too hard to be fair usually end up being extremely unfair, because they ignore individual differences. It is more fair to spend five minutes with a student who needs only five minutes and fifteen minutes with a student who needs fifteen minutes than it is to spend ten minutes with each one.

SUMMARY

Helping, doing for others, providing special attention — teachers and parents tend to see these things as being good. Unnecessary help and attention, however, can easily encourage dependent, irresponsible behavior. It is easy to see students as less capable, less responsible, and less competent than they are. Rushing in to help students who can or who need to help themselves ends with students feeling discouraged about their own abilities to solve problems.

Teachers and parents feel discouraged as well as frustrated when students demand help and attention that they don't really want to give but feel like they must because it's their job as parents or teachers. Such help leaves both adults and children feeling resentful.

Children (and adults) need help and attention that encourages their self-confidence and competence in coping with life. At times giving encouragement requires that we refrain from rushing in to help. At other times, encouragement may require making an exception or making special arrangements which allow students to help themselves. The myths about teaching and parenting we have all been raised with make it difficult to avoid special service.

3
chapter

Fear of Failure

On the day of a big exam, you are horrified as you realize that you've slept through the exam. A feeling of fear and dread comes over you, and then you wake up, relieved that it was only a dream. Many people have this dream long after they have left school. The fear of failure that children experience in school (and out of school) is often not very dramatic and thus doesn't seem serious to adults, yet the prevalence in adults of dreams that deal with school failure should convince us that the fear of failure in school is real.

Fear of failure is fear for self-image. The fear of negative physical consequences (cutting a finger, falling off a bicycle, ruining something) is usually insignificant when compared to the fears that relate to self-image:

- Fear of not measuring up to expectations.
- Fear of looking stupid.
- Fear of humiliation.
- Fear of disapproval.
- Fear of not looking good.
- Fear of getting the wrong answer.
- Fear of making a bad impression.

Loss of status, loss of face, loss of a good opinion, loss of others' approval: These are the things we fear. We find ways of protecting ourselves, but they don't always work well. In school, students also find ways of protecting themselves, but the ways they find often make real learning all but impossible.

Even students who make good grades find themselves concerned much more with avoiding humiliation than with learning. I remember the frustration I experienced as a high school math student. Although my grades were a little above average, I had the feeling that I didn't really know what I was doing. I had no confidence that I really understood math, and I felt that I had been lucky to get by without understanding. In my mind I knew I was not a good math student, no matter what my grades were, and I was afraid that I was dumb, that I couldn't measure up, and that I just had no mind for math.

Living in a culture that puts great emphasis on success generates pressure on students to do well, to avoid mistakes, to win, to be on top. Fear of failure leads to feeling miserable and confused. Fear of failure leads to a loss of confidence, a loss of the feeling that "I can do it," and a loss of trust in oneself to make judgments. In the following paragraphs, a student writes about her own fear of failure and its negative effects:

I've always felt pressured to do well in school. By the time I got to college, I actually got physically sick before tests. After a year of this, one of my teachers sat down with me and explained that getting sick over grades is just not worth it. Now I'm just the opposite

to the extreme: I don't care anymore. To contradict myself, sometimes I still care, and then at other times, I feel like it's not worth it.

The pressure she writes about — pressure from teachers and parents
and the student herself — does not lead to doing well but to doing
poorly:

In my high school, during chorus competition I was so scared and so
afraid of starting early that during a trio I did start early. The pressure built up so much that I was actually relieved by my mistake.

When I'm pressured, I completely lose concentration in classes; and
in high school, when I would be called on for an answer, I would
sometimes just go blank. I would feel like everyone was looking at
me, and suddenly everything would be quiet, and my mind would
just say over and over, "Think of the answer, you dummy." I'm sure
it was the lack of self-confidence that affected me. In high school, I
was so afraid of not being accepted that the pressure built up until
I was so afraid of making mistakes that I did make them. Those
years in high school were pure hell for me, and it still affects me to
this day. I still feel insecure about how people treat me, and I sus-
pect the smallest hint of sarcasm as a blow to me personally.

Sometimes I feel so dumb. This is a very negative statement about
myself, but it's meant to be. It's the negative feeling that comes
along with failure. When I do poorly on a test, I feel so stupid. I
either blame myself and get even more depressed, or I make up
excuses and blame it on my teacher.

Even winning and being successful does not always help the fear of
failure. We can't always be successful, and the experience of success may make failure even more devastating because of unrealistic
expectations. The essay on fear of failure continues as follows:

I can't stand this fear of failure. Ever since I can remember I have
been a winner as far as sports are concerned. This was one of my
great feelings of success. I was always in first place with a trophy or
a medal. Then I started to fail. This upset me to no end. I could not
stand to be beat (I still can't), and when I lost in a game, I would

pout. In high school, I started to fail more often. To ease my feeling
of failure, I made up excuses and gained weight. In high school, I
actually gained ten pounds after an unsuccessful year of track.

What made these experiences failures was the fact that she felt she
was a failure. She's not talking about failing an exam or a course
but rather that she didn't meet her own or her parents' and teachers' expectations. For many students, fear of failure is not fear of
failing exams but the fear of not being a success, of not measuring
up to expectations. Parents, in their concern for their children, can
put pressure on their children that discourages them:

> Parents don't realize the pain they put their children through. My
> father's always saying things like, "Getting A's are the only way to
> success," or "You're going to have to support a husband some day
> so you better go to veterinary school." I personally don't want to be
> a vet, and it hurts me that I can't please my father. I have to deal
> with this stress daily, and I just don't know how long I can take
> it. This pressure leads to failure, if he only knew it. He never thinks
> to praise me when I do well. He just emphasizes my mistakes,
> and this depresses me more. Once when I took a very hard test,
> I got what I thought was a good grade in comparison with the
> other students. My score was an 84.5, and when I told my Dad, he
> just said, "B's aren't good enough, try to do better." I did do my
> best, and his statement really discouraged me and reinforced my
> feeling of failure.

She concludes by talking about herself now:

> Now it's hard for me to feel good about myself. I'm just not trying
> as hard as I used to. It's true that once you get this feeling of failure
> it's hard to change your opinion of yourself.

The feelings of discouragement described by this student
might seem extreme or unusual. They aren't. Over and over I have
seen teachers and parents read essays such as this one and identify
with the experiences they are reading about.

Identifying one's own experiences with fear of failure can help teachers and parents become sensitive to the discouragement children often feel. What makes this example so typical is that the pressure to do well came about out of the best of intentions.

MYTHS ABOUT FEAR OF FAILURE

Teachers and parents act in good faith but often don't realize the consequences of their actions. Many of the common beliefs about motivating students to do well are myths—myths that are powerful because we continue to act as if they were true.

Myth #1: It's Better to Try and Fail
Than Not to Try at All

This may be true for those of us who have had enough success not to be discouraged by failure, but people who constantly experience failure often feel that it's better just to not try; then they don't have to feel bad when they fail again.

Myth #2: Fear of Failure is Caused by a
Few Misguided Teachers and Parents

Certainly some students do develop fear of failure as a result of ridicule, humiliation, or punishment at the hands of an ignorant of even sadistic teacher or parent. Yet if we look at good situations instead of at the worst, we will find that fear of failure is inadvertently encouraged by the well-intentioned efforts of adults to motivate students. This is not a matter of how hard we try or of how good our intentions are. We grow up in a culture that teaches us to use discouragement rather than encouragement as a means of influencing others. It takes a special effort to become aware of the ways we discourage one another and even a greater effort to change.

Myth #3: Fear of Failure
Is a Good Motivator

If you think back to an experience where you applied yourself to a task because you were afraid of doing poorly, it's easy to conclude that fear of failure is a good motivator. Unfortunately, it is also easy to overlook the areas in which we have given up ("I'm no good at math," or "I can't draw a straight line!"). It is easy to overlook the fact that the failures we found motivating were infrequent failures in areas where we were usually successful. For many students, fear of failure does not motivate them because they don't think they can be successful — no matter how hard they try.

Myth #4: Only Poor Students Are Afraid of Failure

On the contrary, good students are often afraid of failure, even in those areas where they are doing quite well. Overambition, encouraged by parents and teachers, may encourage them to feel that they are failures if they aren't first or best in what they do. Pressure on good students does not necessarily help them to learn.

Despite their high grades, many students are afraid of not meeting the expectations of parents and teachers. In many cases, they are not even sure what *is* expected of them. Good students are not necessarily good learners. Good students are likely to avoid asking questions that might make them look stupid. They may be concerned more with their grades than with understanding or learning. They may have a low tolerance for ambiguity; they want to know what the right answer is and may feel frustrated when faced with questions that do not have *one* right answer.

DE-EMPHASIZING FAILURE

Help students put failure into perspective. There are many ways of doing this.

Treat Failure in a Matter-of-fact Way. Don't act shocked when a child fails. Don't preach, harp, nag, or otherwise carry on in an attempt to change the student immediately. Even if you succeed, he or she will not thank you for it. I remember, back in the fourth grade, being treated like a criminal on the road to hell because I was not working very hard and my grades had fallen. My grades did improve, so it worked, I suppose. I was not encouraged to learn or do things but only to stay out of trouble—at which I succeeded fairly well, because I was afraid not to.

De-emphasize Success. Just as it is important to de-emphasize failure, it is equally important not to emphasize success. Success is more likely to be encouraging when it is treated matter-of-factly. Putting emphasis on success only serves to emphasize the possibility of failure.

Admit Mistakes. Treating your own mistakes in an open and matter-of-fact way will encourage students to do likewise.

COPING WITH MISTAKES

As a teacher and parent, I find myself faced with a double bind. If I correct mistakes, I often find myself dealing with a discouraged child or student. If I don't correct mistakes, I'm concerned that the mistakes will be repeated in the future. I find myself recreating the discouragement that was visited on me as a child from my own parents and teachers.

Our culture teaches us to feel self-conscious about mistakes—both those we make ourselves and those we see others make. We find it hard not to see mistakes as failures. Yet what makes mistakes discouraging is that we think of mistakes as failures. Mistakes come to be regarded as failures because we tell ourselves that they are. Students believe that their mistakes represent failure because they have learned to feel bad about them. Learning to feel bad about mistakes doesn't encourage people to avoid mistakes; it only encourages them to avoid looking for mistakes—what Holt (1964) calls the "don't look back" strategy.

The following suggestions are concerned with helping teachers cope with mistakes without creating discouragement.

Expect and Plan for Mistakes. It wasn't until I started doing computer programming that one of my myths about making mistakes completely broke down. I had been encouraged to believe that if I was careful and knew what I was doing, there wouldn't be any mistakes. My experience doing programming was somewhat traumatic until I found out that all computer programs have mistakes the first few times they are run, no matter how careful the programmer.

We need to encourage children to deal with mistakes as a fact of life instead of getting upset by them. Treating mistakes as sins encourages unrealistic expectations. Admonitions such as "There shouldn't be any mistakes," or "Be careful and there won't be any mistakes" encourage students to regard mistakes as personal, moral, or intellectual failures.

Encourage Students to Look for Mistakes. Coping with one's own mistakes takes great peace of mind. One way to avoid becoming upset by mistakes is to celebrate when a mistake is found. *Finding* a mistake is a cause for rejoicing because you can then *do* something about it. Unfortunately, students are so afraid of mistakes (they're really afraid of feeling bad) that they refuse to look over their work.

Encourage Students to Ignore Mistakes Where Appropriate. There are times when mistakes should be ignored. For example, when typing a first draft of a manuscript, I find that I get much more done if I ignore mistakes in typing, spelling, grammar, and punctuation. It slows me down too much to keep correcting the mistakes that creep in — besides, I know I'll correct them on the next draft. When my daughter, age eight at the time, was using a typewriter to type letters to her grandparents, she would get very frustrated because of all the mistakes. I showed her some of my typing and tried to convince her that she didn't need to have her letter perfect. There are times when avoiding and eliminating mistakes need to have high priority. There are times when it's more appropriate to ignore mistakes or to correct mistakes at a later time.

Encourage students to ignore mistakes when they have trouble finishing work because they're discouraged about their mistakes.

Encourage students to ignore mistakes when they're first learning a skill, when they're writing a first draft, or when it's important to finish a task or a performance. One of the first things a young performer must learn is that you keep going, ignoring mistakes, until you are finished.

Don't Make Assignments that Generate Unnecessary Mistakes. Don't make assignments that call for extensive repetition. Try doing a page of arithmetic problems or copying a word or sentence a hundred times. Chances are that you will start making mistakes and that your work will start to deteriorate by the end of the page. Human beings do not function well when asked to repeat the same task over and over. Mistakes crop up and create discouragement. Repetition doesn't enhance learning unless it's meaningful.

Get "Hired" before You Correct Mistakes. No one wants a solution when he doesn't think he has a problem. Parents and teachers often try to help children to correct a mistake when the help isn't wanted. But adult and child end up frustrated by attempts to help when the adult hasn't been "hired" by the child (Gordon, 1974). Children often resent or reject help they haven't asked for or don't want. You know you've been hired by a child when the child willingly accepts your help.

Don't Feel Responsible for Others' Mistakes. Teachers who feel that a student's mistake is a reflection on them are likely to try too hard. Parents are even more likely to discourage their children by trying too hard because they tend to feel responsible for the child's progress. You can be more patient, more objective, and more encouraging by learning to avoid feeling responsible for the mistakes your children make. We feel responsible because of what we've been told and because of what we tell ourselves. Although it is difficult, we can change how we feel by telling ourselves that we're not responsible for others' mistakes.

PRAISE

Praise can be encouraging, but it can also contribute to anxiety and fear of failure. Praise has been oversold as a technique to increase motivation and change behavior. Like all techniques, praise can easily become manipulative and underhanded. Most of us are suspicious when someone praises, and often with good reason. The suggestions that follow are concerned with avoiding the hazards of praise.

Be Honest. Praise that is not honest is likely to backfire. It creates confusion and mistrust, as the seventh-grade teacher in the following example found out:

> This past year, I had a seventh grader who had very poor language skills. I had had his brother the previous year, and he was the same way. I wasn't able to help the older brother to my satisfaction, so I made up my mind to "get to" this one. Praise was going to be my method of encouragement. During their class work, I would make it a point to stop at his desk to see how he was getting along. I would usually say something such as "You're on the right track," or "Keep up the good work." I would usually look at the first few problems or maybe spot check. I didn't want to point out too many errors for fear of discouraging him. Needless to say, it backfired. When his paper was corrected, he usually missed more than half. During a conversation, he asked me why I said he was doing a good job when he was really missing more than half. His self-image as a student didn't match what I had said about him being on the right track.

As the teacher correctly mentions, pointing out too many errors would have been discouraging. On the other hand, the teacher's praise was also discouraging. Working out some realistic goals with the student and then praising him for improvement is an approach that might have worked better. The teacher would then be able to praise the student without pretending that he was doing better than he really was. Denying the reality of a low level of accomplishment does not lead to encouragement; on the other hand, even the student with the most severe problems can feel good about the things that he or she does well and about the progress he or she is making.

Avoid Using Praise to Soften Criticism. How often praise is followed by criticism! When someone says, "You did a good job...," and then pauses, we anticipate "but...," followed by criticism.

Avoid Using Praise to Pressure Students. "You always do so well!" often becomes transformed into pressure to do well all the time. Because of such pressure, some students feel discouraged by praise because they're afraid they won't be able to repeat their success.

Be Careful: Praise May Be Resented. Praise can be condescending, maintaining the superiority of one person over another, in which case it is likely to be resented. Students may also resent praise when it isolates them from their peers by singling them out or by embarrassing them.

Be Slow to Praise, because Praise Is an Evaluation. A positive evaluation is still an evaluation, and many people are uncomfortable with evaluations, whether positive or negative. Another problem that arises is that students who are used to being praised may feel that they have been given a negative evaluation simply because the teacher neglected to praise them. Finally, some students may feel that they don't deserve praise and thus may feel anxious when someone praises them — especially if the praise exaggerates their accomplishments.

When You Praise, Praise Those Who Need It. Praise is most likely to go to those students who need it least. Praising only those who have achieved a certain superiority is likely to encourage students to feel superior and the poor students to feel inferior.

Don't Push Positive Thinking. When a student feels upset or discouraged, don't try to humor the student with positive thinking ("You can do it," and similar expressions). Respecting students' feelings will be more encouraging in the long run.

APPRECIATION

Expressing appreciation means sharing personal feelings with another person. Here are some examples:

- "I appreciate your friendship."
- "I enjoy the way you read."
- "I appreciate your cheerfulness."
- "I appreciate you for the way you keep plugging away."
- "I enjoy the way you use color so freely in your pictures."

Appreciation may seem to be the same thing as praise, but there are important differences. Praise is an evaluation: "You're doing a good job." Appreciation is an expression of feeling: "I appreciate the work you're doing." In the first case, I'm stating a fact; in the second case, I'm sharing something of myself. Praise is usually concerned with recognizing excellence, superiority, or high achievement. Appreciation is a positive regard: "I enjoy watching you," "I like you," "I appreciate you." When you use the pronoun "I" in "I like you" or "I appreciate you," you take a risk: You share something of yourself.

COMPETITION

Competition, especially competition that involves loss of face, humiliation, or continued failure, often creates anxiety and fear of failure.

A level of anxiety or fear may be motivating to some students in some situations. In general, however, overconcern for success and fear of failure both interfere with functioning. We can't do two things at once. Worry, fear, anxiety, and frustration: Any of these feelings can become the focus of attention, and when they do, learning suffers.

Because competition is so much a part of schooling—and to some people's minds, a basic part of our whole way of life—we need to look at some of the myths that are used to defend competition in school. To be sure, there is competition in life — on the job, in sports, and at play — yet the competition that we meet as adults is often quite different from the competition that children face in school.

Myth #1: Competition Prepares
Students for Life

Adults are seldom faced with the daily threats to their self-image that face many children. Also, adults are allowed to choose, to some extent, the level on which they wish to compete or even to choose whether they wish to compete. Adults are allowed the dignity of selecting their own goals.

Myth #2: Competition
Motivates Students

Competition motivates only those students who feel that they have a chance of doing well. Those who feel they have no chance simply give up.

Myth #3: Competition Is the American
Way — Look at Sports!

Whenever I bring up arguments against competition in school, the sports-minded bring up sports, which they then proceed to defend. A look at sports, however, will, I believe, show that unlimited competition is not encouraged or even allowed in sports. A great deal of effort is made in sports to avoid competition between individuals who are mismatched. Consider the following:

- In public schools, conferences are matched according to size of schools in an effort to create balanced conferences.

- In college, conferences are organized on the basis of size and overall athletic strength of a school in a particular sport.

- In professional sports, special rules prevent (or attempt to prevent) one team from buying all the best players and therefore dominating a league. Admittedly, this does not always work, but the care that goes into regulating draft choices and trades is an obvious example of this. Grossly mismatched teams are not interesting to watch.

Myth #4: People Should Be Encouraged to Compete Against Themselves

No doubt some people have pushed themselves to higher levels of performance by competing against themselves, but they are usually successful in this endeavor in one area, not in everything they do. Even with such people, what do they do when they have reached their peak and cannot get any better? They are then faced with the problem of what to do. Competing against yourself may make sense for certain people in certain situations, but it discourages people from doing many things they would like to do simply because they are afraid they won't measure up to their own expectations.

Myth #5: Students Won't Be Able to Deal with Competition When They Grow Up if They Don't Have to Compete in School

Just the opposite may be true. People who concentrate on doing a job are likely to do better than those who are overly concerned about how they're doing. The person who has one eye on the competition seldom does well. Forcing students to compete encourages them to worry about how they're doing instead of focusing on doing a job.

USING COMPETITION

Competition can be enjoyable and stimulating when it does not lead to a feeling of failure on the part of the loser or a feeling of superiority on the part of the winner. Usually, such times are limited to situations where the participants care much more about the activity than they do about winning. Unfortunately, few of us are able to care more about the activity than about winning. In summary, if you use competition, remember the following:

- Focus on the activity, not on winning or losing.
- Don't over-reward winning or over-emphasize losing.
- Keep competition among equals; don't match individuals where one doesn't have a chance.
- Make participation voluntary and provide alternate activities for those who don't want to participate.
- Emphasize the cooperative aspects of competition.

Many forms of competition won't fit these guidelines, and some that do fit the guidelines will not be appropriate for certain individuals. For example, checkers may be a good way for some children to spend their time, but not for those who insist on winning. Spelling bees, on the other hand, violate most of the guidelines most of the time and are thus a poor way of encouraging learning, except perhaps, for those few students who are successful.

SUMMARY

Fear of failure is a universal experience in our culture. The pressure that teachers and parents put on children to do well, to succeed, and to win are well-intentioned but serve to discourage students. We are taught to believe that pressure to do well and fear of failure are good motivators, but observation shows that they lead more often to discouragement. The experience of failure seldom encourages students to do better.

Mistakes are not failures but facts of life to be dealt with. Mistakes can be discouraging, but by helping students to adopt rational and realistic attitudes about mistakes, mistakes can be occasions for learning instead of for discouragement. Praise and competition, two other time-honored ways of motivating students to do well, can easily become pressures that generate discouragement and fear of failure.

Fear of failure is image-centered. It is fear for our self-image we or others have of ourselves. In the past, threats to self-image were thought to be the way to motivate people. Instilling fear of failure, emphasizing mistakes, and using praise and competition to pressure both children and adults were thought to be the best way to encourage excellence, competence, success, and even happiness. Becoming aware of the extent to which these methods create discouragement is the first step in changing to methods that are more encouraging. Help students put their fears, mistakes, and even failures into a proper perspective. Emphasize both success and failure by teaching students to cope with problems and mistakes, by emphasizing problem solving, and by avoiding threats to self-image.

4
chapter

Student Strategies

Survival in school means avoiding humiliation, loss of face, low grades, dirty looks from teachers or fellow students, criticism from parents, or the dreaded feeling of failure. Students invent strategies to survive: One student mumbles so that the teacher will pass him by; another invents explanations rather than admit that she doesn't understand; a third student looks puzzled when he isn't. These are strategies—purposeful actions designed for survival.

John Holt wrote about the strategies his students used in *How Children Fail* (1964). As a teacher of in-service teachers, I began assigning *How Children Fail*, and teachers in my classes began talking about strategies they had noticed in their own classes after they had read Holt. It seemed that the hardest part of coping with student strategies was being aware of them in the first place. Once the teachers were familiar with the idea of strategies and had seen a few examples, they quickly identified strategies in their own classrooms. The thirteen strategies described here have been distilled from hundreds of examples observed by teachers. They aren't a complete map of the territory, but they do serve as signposts indicating where to look for strategies.

1. GOOD SOLDIER SCHWIEK

When you're a student, the Schwiek strategy goes like this:

- Look like you're trying.
- Look like you're busy.
- Look like you know the answer and then look confused if called on.

Schweik was a folk hero celebrated in a novel written around the time of World War I and later made into an opera called "Good Soldier Schwiek." Schwiek always did everything he was told to do, yet he always managed to do the wrong thing. He appeared to be so simple and so well intentioned that his commanding officer didn't know what to do with him. By "playing stupid," he was able to sabotage the efforts of those around him without really getting into trouble. Some students are so good at playing stupid while having good intentions that no one suspects that they are capable of doing far more.

Sometimes it takes a while to catch on to a Schwiek strategy. Recently, while discussing a sixteen-year-old male student I was counseling with his teacher, the teacher said, "Do you ever have the feeling someone is looking at you, and then when you look up, no one is?" Ted, the student in question, was a master at looking busy without being so. This was not so much a result of laziness as it was of discouragement. Ted didn't want to talk about or even think about school. He had been sitting in high-school math classes without being able to do second-grade arithmetic.

Suggestions for Coping. Assigning tasks that are too long or too complex leads to discouragement and "Schwieking." What's too long or too complex depends on the individual. My daughter, age nine, will make her bed without assistance, but when she is told to clean up her messy room, she feels overwhelmed and sloughs off after picking up a few things. Breaking down a complex task into several simple assignments sometimes works well in this kind of situation.

Make goals very specific. Discuss work in terms of specific tasks and how they can be accomplished, not in terms of how hard the student tried or how busy he or she looked.

Be careful in judging what a student can do. If you feel Johnny tries hard, but he just can't seem to get it, maybe Johnny is having trouble — but maybe he's also Schwieking in order to avoid unpleasant tasks and to make you think he's working harder than he is.

2. "I DON'T UNDERSTAND."

A student using this strategy might describe it this way:

- If at first you don't succeed, tell the teacher you don't understand.
- When directions are given by the teacher, raise your hand and say, "I don't understand."
- Don't hear directions the first time. Ask the teacher to repeat them.

Phrases such as "I don't understand" often keep teachers busy giving explanations or repeating directions. This example is based on the experience of an art teacher working in a summer arts program:

The art teacher was working with forty or more students. One child never seemed to understand directions, even when the others had no trouble. At first, the teacher tried explaining, but no matter how many times she explained, the child replied, "Show me how to do it," or "I don't understand." The teacher had too many students to continue this special service, and so she let the child alone. For a week, the child stood around looking puzzled. Finally, she began to work on her own, and the teacher soon noticed that the child could grasp the instructions as well as anyone.

Suggestions for Coping. When teachers recognize this strategy, they may want to consider one of the following alternatives:

- Don't jump to rescue the student. Immediate offers of help may only reinforce dependence on the teacher's help.
- Don't do projects for the student.
- Use reflective listening followed by silence. Comments such as "You don't understand," or "You aren't sure what to do" let students know that you've heard them, but they also keep the responsibility for the problem where it belongs — on the student (see Chapter 5, *Communication*).
- Offer a compromise where you think it's appropriate. For example: "I'm willing to look at your work after you get a start on it." The idea is not simply to abandon the student but to insist that he or she do what he or she can do before the teacher provides help.

3. USING QUESTIONS

Faced with the problem of answering a teacher's question, some students use this strategy in order to turn the tables:

- Narrow down an answer by asking questions such as "Do you mean. . .or do you mean. . . ?" Once you're on the right track, you may be able to guess the answer.
- When a teacher asks a question, answer with a question. Many teachers can't resist answering a question, and you'll get off the hook, at least temporarily.

Here is an example shared by a male high school teacher about
one of his students:

> Don was a blind student in a regular high school science class. He
> could have taken his tests in Braille, but the teacher did not prepare
> the tests far enough in advance to have them translated. Teacher and
> student agreed on oral exams. When the teacher asked a question,
> Don asked for clarifications: Which aspect of the question did the
> teacher want Don to discuss? Was the teacher thinking of this or
> that? And so on. Don did very well.

The teacher commented in an assignment that he had never
realized that he had been manipulated into giving Don the main
points of most of the answers. Since Don was a bright student,
no wonder he was able to fill in the details once the teacher had
been led to indicate the main points!

Don was not seen as a problem since he was a good student;
none of his teachers realized that they were being manipulated
during his oral exams. Don was unusual in that he was blind, but
the strategy of shaping the teacher's questions to reveal the answer
is a common one.

Suggestions for Coping. Tape-record yourself in order to find
out how you answer questions. Once you become aware of
what you are saying and doing, you can change what you feel is
appropriate.

Don't answer questions if you feel you'll be giving away more
than you want to or if you feel the question is a way of avoiding
responsibility. There's no right way to do this, but here are several
alternatives:

STUDENT: "What do you mean? I'm not sure what you want."

TEACHER: "You're not sure what to do." Or, "You're not sure
what I want." Or, "You're confused."

All of the teacher responses above put the responsibility back

on the student to respond to the teacher's original question. The
teacher responses are simply reflecting back what the student has
said — without putting down the student.

Here are some other alternatives:

STUDENT: "What do you mean?"

TEACHER: "I'd like to hear your ideas before I say anything
          else." Or, "Tell us what you think about the ques-
          tion." Or, "What do you think the person who asked
          the question might have had in mind?"

These responses by the teacher put the responsibility for interpreting the question back on the student. The goal in all these
responses is to make teaching an interaction rather than a
monologue. The more the teacher talks and explains and answers
his or her own questions, the less the students are involved in the
learning process.

Finally, keep in mind that, at times, giving an explanation may
be called for. There are times when teachers do need to explain
further. On the other hand, most teachers spend too much time
talking and explaining, and students know how to encourage this
tendency, thus getting themselves off the hook.

4. WAITING FOR APPROVAL

This strategy is used most often by discouraged students who
feel unsure of themselves:

- Wait for the teacher to say "O.K.," "Go on," "That's
  right," or "Good!" before you go on to the next word or
  the next problem. Do nothing until she does.

Students who use this strategy refuse to do anything until the
teacher tells them that their work is O.K. or that they've gotten

the right answer. Teachers sometimes inadvertently encourage this strategy in the belief that immediate feedback and approval are always desirable. The practice of giving immediate reinforcement may be a good idea in general, but it can lead to dependency. Some time ago, a special education teacher and I watched a tape she had made of her teaching. We discovered that one of her students, a boy who had difficulties reading, stopped after every word, waiting for the teacher to say "Right—go on," or "Good!" The teacher reinforced the child's behavior because she didn't realize what was happening. She was an excellent teacher and was surprised when she saw the videotape.

Suggestions for Coping. Be patient. Becoming angry or frustrated will only make a child more reluctant to go on without your approval. Don't correct every mistake; this interrupts students when your goal is to get the student to work more steadily. Ignore bids for approval where possible. If a student is waiting for you to say O.K., say nothing. Eventually, he or she will realize that you're not going to say O.K. any more and will stop waiting for you.

5. LOOKING PUZZLED

Looking puzzled can be a useful strategy for getting help and special attention—even if they aren't really needed:

- If you don't know what to do, look at the teacher as if she just said something that sounds crazy.
- When playing a musical instrument in band and you make a mistake, stare at the music as if it contains a mistake. Alternately, look at your instrument as if it isn't working properly.
- Make sure that the teacher sees you when you look puzzled.

Even when students *are* puzzled, looking puzzled can be a strategy to avoid responsibility for working on a task. Looking puzzled invites the teacher to help—and getting help may be easier and more attractive to a student than struggling with a problem.

Suggestions for Coping. Not every student who looks puzzled is using a strategy. This behavior becomes a strategy when it is consistently used as a way of getting unnecessary help. Monitor your own behavior in order to determine whether you're providing unnecessary help that encourages dependence. Ignore looking puzzled if it's a bid for unnecessary help. Not providing unnecessary help for a student who is used to it is a positive action—and, sometimes, not an easy one.

6. MINIMIZING LOSSES

There are many ways students minimize their chances of being wrong. Here are two of the most common:

- Hedge. Never give a direct answer if you can help it.
- Never take a stand. Then you can't be told you're wrong.

These strategies are ways of minimizing loss of face. Students who fear being wrong or being put down use these strategies to protect themselves. Holt (1964) calls this the "minimax" strategy: Maximize your gain; minimize your losses. If you never come out in a direct way, you can never be completely wrong.

What Holt found was that some of his students were afraid not to be right because they had no confidence in themselves. A wrong answer was a personal defeat, a sign of inferiority. Answering a question was not a means of learning but a threat to self-image.

Suggestions for Coping. Students use these strategies because they have been put down or because they have learned to feel stupid or afraid when they are wrong. Whenever a question is a threat to an individual's self-image, the minimax strategy is likely to come into play. One way to discourage this strategy is not to make a fuss about either wrong answers or right answers.

Be careful about giving your own opinion in discussion periods. Many students are reluctant to give their own opinions unless they know what the teacher's opinion is, especially if that teacher is likely to argue or show disapproval if the student disagrees.

7. GUESSING EXPLANATIONS

When students are asked for explanations, they may use one of these strategies:

- When asked to explain something you don't understand, pretend that you know and make a guess. If you use the same words the teacher used, you may get by, even if you get them mixed up.
- For teachers who insist that you "show your work," show at least some work on assignments; even if you don't know what you're doing, it will look like you're trying, and maybe you'll get partial credit.

We assume that explanation shows understanding, yet explanations are often given without being understood by students in order to satisfy a teacher's desire to have an explanation. They feel that they must please their teachers; they're afraid not to. The following example is based on a composite of many examples by college students who remembered how they got around math teachers who insisted that students show their work.

A conscientious math teacher wanted students to understand what they were doing and would not give credit for a problem unless students showed their work. Many students who were afraid of not getting credit put elaborate figuring in the margins, even if they didn't know how to work a problem. The teacher, anxious to help students, diligently corrected tests without realizing that what he read didn't always represent a genuine effort.

This situation must be common. I can remember taking math tests in high school and putting down some work for each problem — even if I didn't know how to solve the problem — in hopes of getting at least some credit.

Grading only answers is no solution, either. It is important for students to understand what they're doing, and getting a right answer does not necessarily indicate understanding. The point that John Holt makes in *How Children Fail* (1964) is that explanations do not necessarily indicate understanding and that teachers need to be careful when they accept explanations or when they pressure students to give explanations.

Suggestions for Coping. Pressure for explanations can produce an emphasis on explanation — any explanation — instead of on understanding. De-emphasize getting the "right" explanation. Avoid pressure. Few students (or teachers, for that matter) can think when faced with an audience of twenty-five or more people waiting for their answer.

Ask students to give explanations and definitions in their own words. Good students may memorize an answer without knowing what it means. Explanations can also be memorized.

Ask for examples or applications from experience. Memorizing an example from a book is quite different than giving an example from one's own experience. Holt gives an example in *How Children Fail* (1964) of a class where students have learned that the core of the earth is in a state of igneous fusion, but the students have no idea of what igneous fusion means, nor can they describe the earth's core in terms that relate to their own experience.

Avoid giving credit for work you don't understand, or you may be encouraging meaningless explanations that have been invented for your benefit. Giving credit for work that doesn't make sense, in the belief that students who try hard should be encouraged, doesn't work.

8. WHISPERING AND MUMBLING

Some students whisper or mumble answers in an effort to be as inconspicuous as possible (Holt, 1964). If they could, they might describe their strategy as follows:

- When reading aloud and you come to a word you don't know, lower your voice and mumble.
- When your teacher asks a question, answer the question, but not loud enough to be heard.
- When you're not sure of the answer, mumble something that includes the appropriate words (you can usually tell the appropriate words from the question).

Strategies such as these serve to discourage the teacher from calling on a student. The teacher stops being aware that there is a problem.

Many college students I have worked with have told stories about themselves very much like the one in the following example:

> It was a middle-elementary school class. June would raise her hand, at times waving it enthusiastically in the air, but when she was called on, she could barely be heard. The teacher would often pick up on a word or two and expand on June's "right" answer.

Suggestions for Coping. Don't call on students in order to humiliate or punish them. Don't push too hard. On the other hand, don't answer questions yourself: Wait for an answer. Silence will encourage student responses, whereas immediately answering questions yourself will discourage student responses. In an ordinary conversation, a lapse of even two seconds of silence between speakers is unusual and leads to a feeling of uneasiness that causes the participants to overestimate the amount of wait time involved. Learning to wait for students to respond is difficult, but it will increase both the quantity and quality of student responses (Rowe, 1974). Here are some ways of increasing your wait time:

- Don't feel responsible for the silence. Feeling responsible for the silence increases the feeling that you have to speak if no one else does.
- Count off seconds to yourself silently.
- Use a watch to time silences if you can do so without being obvious.
- Tape-record yourself, and then check how long you wait for students to answer before answering yourself or calling on someone else.

9. THE ANSWER ON TEACHER'S FACE

Many students use a strategy that goes like this:

- Watch for nonverbal hints from the teacher and change your answer accordingly. Here are some examples of what to look for:

  Teacher knits brow or makes a sour face.

  Teacher looks encouraging; nods head up and down.

  Teacher stands near the answer on the blackboard.

  Teacher frowns or smiles as the student is giving an answer.

Teachers communicate what they're looking for through facial expressions. I can remember one of my teachers staring down a boy who didn't know an answer and then saying in an irritated tone of voice, "Why are you looking at me? The answer isn't written on my forehead!" Without realizing it, the teacher had in fact spoken the truth — or close to it: The student was looking for nonverbal cues from the teacher's face.

Suggestions for Coping. Are you unintentionally giving cues to students? Maybe they're looking for an answer — and finding it. A teacher's expression can also discourage students from answering at all.

What feels like a very small facial movement causes a very noticeable change of expression. Stand in front of a mirror. Close your eyes, and then raise or lower your eyebrows as little as possible. Repeat the experiment, this time watching yourself in a mirror. What feels like a minimal movement results in a very visible change. Once you become aware of what a particular expression feels like, you can monitor your expressions even though you can't see yourself.

Changing attitudes can also be useful in avoiding nonverbal cues that give away answers or that discourage students from answering at all. Nonverbal cues are often indications of feelings of approval or disapproval. By avoiding feelings of approval or disapproval when students answer questions or express opinions, you can eliminate inappropriate expressions of approval or disapproval.

Facial expressions, especially those of disapproval, can easily be interpreted by students as unacceptance of them rather than just as indications of a right or wrong answer. Also, if teachers show disapproval when students say something the teacher doesn't want to hear, the student is likely to stop talking altogether—which can be a problem, because teachers need to know what's getting across and what students are thinking and feeling. Expressions of approval can also have the same effect, because they may give the impression that a teacher is being unaccepting when approval is not given.

We feel disapproval when we tell ourselves that a student *should* be better prepared, *should* know the answer, or *should* have different ideas. By realizing that we are making ourselves feel disapproval, we can change our feelings. Changing these feelings is not easy, but it can be accomplished with practice. These feelings are a matter of habit — like getting mad at a red light because the car in front of you doesn't start fast enough when the light turns green. Once you realize that you, not the car in front of you, are responsible for how you feel, you can change.

Particularly in group discussions, I've noticed that if I'm not careful, expressions of either approval or disapproval of what is being said can change what students will say. Approval can create almost as much inhibition as disapproval, because once students catch on to what's being approved, many will say only what they think will meet with my approval. What students are really concerned about is acceptance: If they feel accepted and worthwhile, they are more willing to be concerned with the subject at hand rather than with their self-images.

10. HAND-RAISING STRATEGIES

Students faced with being called on may rely on these strategies:

- If a teacher likes to call on students who aren't prepared, raise your hand and look confident. You probably won't be called on.
- If you *want* to be called on, look confused or puzzled and don't raise your hand. When the teacher calls on you and you know the answer, will he or she be in for a surprise!

Perhaps the only way teachers can discourage these strategies is by avoiding a teacher-centered classroom. As long as a teacher is the focus of attention, students are likely to use hand-raising strategies. Here's how one person described a personal experience with hand-raising strategies:

I always felt like I was the center of attention because I sat in the middle row, in the second seat from the teacher's desk. My teacher seemed to use the strategy of calling on students who seemed to be confused or who were not paying attention in class. Therefore, I felt pretty secure raising my hand when a question was asked, whether I knew the answer or not. This seemed to indicate that at least I knew what was going on, and it seemed to lessen the chances of being called on.

Suggestions for Coping. Use teaching methods that don't require answering questions in a large group. Many students feel pressured when they have to speak in front of a group of twenty-five or more other students. When you do call on students, be systematic. Research indicates that in classes where teachers do not have a systematic procedure for calling on students, some students are almost never called on, whereas others are called on relatively frequently.

Going around the room can be a useful technique, especially if students are sitting in a circle for discussion. Overuse of this technique can inhibit discussion, however, and may encourage students to stop paying attention when they have answered. Teachers can memorize two or three patterns for calling on students in order to avoid going around the room. For example, a teacher might call on students by using a diagonal pattern, by starting in the middle of the room and working outward, or by starting at the back and working forward.

11. CRAM AND MEMORIZE

- Cram for teachers who call for rote memorization on tests. You'll probably do just as well or better than students who have been reading the book along with the teacher.

The problem with cramming is that material that is learned for a test and never used again is quickly forgotten. Some of my students have claimed that they have found themselves forgetting even before the test is over! Like the waiter who can remember everything on your bill—until you've paid—students can often learn large amounts of information without having any intention of retaining that information. This example is from my own experience:

> I remember very well a course in graduate school. I attended all the
> lectures and enjoyed them, but I didn't get around to reading the

book. There was one exam — a one-hundred item true-false test.
Reading the text through once the day before the test was sufficient
to earn one of the highest scores in the class.

Suggestions for Coping. As long as teachers create situations where
cramming pays off, students will make use of a wide variety of
cramming and memorizing techniques that do not lead to long-
term retention or use. Of course, not everything needs to be re-
tained for long periods of time, but then why insist that students
spend large blocks of time learning material that will be forgotten
after a test? Like many strategies, cramming is a way students
adapt to a learning structure set by the teacher. If teachers change
the structure so that such strategies no longer pay off, students
will give them up because they are no longer effective.

Restructuring a class is a large topic in itself. Here are some
changes that can be effective:

- Use forms of evaluation other than exams. Projects,
  presentations, papers, and group work can provide opportunities for evaluation without rewarding cramming or
  memorizing.

- Avoid true-false and multiple-choice tests, or make them
  a minor part of evaluation and grading.

- Use forms of evaluation that require students to show or
  describe applications of what they've learned — especially
  if those applications relate to their own experience.

12. LOWERING
ADULT EXPECTATIONS

- If a teacher grades on improvement, be sure to do poorly
  on the first test so that the teacher will be pleasantly surprised when you do better than expected.

- If the work is too hard or too much, and if there are other
  classes or groups that are not expected to do as much or to

do as well, be sure to do poorly so that you may be sent to a "lower ability" group.

- Do poorly on ability tests. Teachers and parents may not expect as much.

The following example is based on an episode one of my students told about himself and how he managed to avoid being placed in a "high ability" class.

A seventh-grade teacher was attempting to motivate her students just before they began a standardized ability test. She pointed out that their scores would determine which teacher they would be placed with during the next year. One boy realized that if he did too well, he would be placed in the advanced class and would have to work harder for less recognition. He deliberately did poorly, and the next year, he was the top student in the "low ability" class. He was too successful, however, and was transferred to the more advanced class. He stopped studying, made poor grades, and was demoted back to the first class where he once again did well, pleasing his relieved parents by making the honor roll.

This boy's strategy may be seen as an example of laziness where a student got by with doing as little as possible. On the other hand, this student's strategy can be seen as an attempt to cope with the demands of parents and teachers to be successful.

Suggestions for Coping. By overemphasizing being first or being special, teachers and parents may discourage an interest in learning. In the case just mentioned, what the student did made good sense from his point of view. He could be special in the lower group. In the upper group, he might have learned more and might even have found the challenge interesting, but he would have been just an average student in a class of good students. Some teachers might feel that this boy was merely lazy and didn't want to work. Yet laziness is usually a form of discouragement. The person who acts lazy may feel that he or she can't be special or be first, so why should he or she try? By emphasizing specialness, we teach children to evaluate tasks in terms of the opportunity to be special, to be first, or to be on top.

What steps can a teacher take?

- Avoid overmotivation. Don't make an issue of how important a test is. A moderate amount of motivation works better than either too much or too little.
- Avoid comparing students with one another. The pep talk the teacher mentioned above gave to her students encouraged those students who didn't do well to think of themselves as second best — that is, as losers.
- Don't encourage specialness. The important thing is learning as much as possible, not being first, smartest, or best.
- Be careful about your expectations of slower groups or slower students. Expecting less work or a lower quality of work may encourage students to live *down* to your expectations. Of course, expectations that are too high will tend to end in frustration and discouragement for both teacher and students.
- Encourage parents to de-emphasize specialness and to take an interest in the student's learning rather than in how well he or she did in comparison to others.

13. SOUR GRAPES

- Criticize something if you aren't sure you can do it.
- Get off the defensive by putting your teacher on the defensive. Ask questions, such as, "Why do we have to do this?" or make complaints, such as, "This is dumb!"

Criticizing is sometimes a way of trying to get out of doing something you aren't sure you can do. This example comes from my experience in high-school band:

The high-school band was having a rough time with a new piece of music. Finally, one boy said to another, in a whisper loud enough for the band director to hear, "This is a corny piece." The director stopped, looked the speaker squarely in the eye, and said in an irritated but gentle way, "Son, don't knock it if you can't play it."

The band director addressed the real issue — playing the piece. In the following example, a similar situation is described by an art teacher:

When I did my student-teaching, I was teaching a class the techniques involved in macramé (the art of tying knots). Everything was going along really well. The students caught on quickly and were really interested in the project they were working on.

Then, one day, a new student was transferred in. He was loud, obnoxious, and, to say the least, he interrupted the other students who were diligently working on their wall hangings. He informed me that the assignment was "dumb" and "stupid." I gave him some personal attention, since he was really behind the other students. Although his attitude had been extremely poor when he first arrived, it changed as he accomplished each knot we had learned. I later found out that he had been afraid to attempt macramé because it appears to be delicate. He felt that he would be too clumsy to achieve the effects the other students had accomplished.

In one of Aesop's fables, a fox tries to reach a bunch of grapes that are too high for him. He excuses himself for not getting the grapes by claiming that the grapes were sour anyway. Students who feel discouraged may complain or criticize an assignment as being silly, dumb, or stupid when they are actually afraid of failing.

Suggestions for Coping

- Listen to the student's underlying message: Is it discouragement? Aggressive behavior may be a way to cover insecurity.

- Suggest what the real message may be. For example, "You're not sure whether you can do the assignment," or "It's tough right now to get this assignment done on time."

- Don't take criticism personally. Once a teacher recognizes that the criticism may be a strategy to cover up insecurity, it's much easier to avoid feeling defensive.

- Keep in mind that even though the criticism may be a strategy, it may also be true. Many assignments are dumb or silly. If, after thinking the matter over, you agree with the student, simply admit it and make a new assignment. "You're right, that assignment is silly, let's do something else" is a statement that can only come from a secure, courageous teacher.

SUMMARY

A college student who read the examples of strategies described here summarized his own experience very well by saying, "When I was in high school and all the way through college, I worked hard to 'figure out' the teacher. Once I knew what he or she wanted, it was easy to do just that and then to make the grade."

The suggestions given to discourage strategies can be summarized as follows:

- Become aware of strategies. You can't do anything about a situation you're not aware of.

- Change your own behavior. Listen. Don't inadvertently reinforce strategies.

- Change classroom structure. Changes in assignments, grouping, testing, or grading can be used to discourage particular strategies.

There is no way to discourage students from using strategies as long as students are pressured to meet expectations of teachers and parents that focus on getting right answers and good grades rather than on understanding and competence. Strategies are a survival response—a way to protect one's self-image. This doesn't mean that teachers and parents should lower their expectations of what students can do. Just the opposite. Many students can do far more than they are now expected to do.

Coping with strategies—I don't think they can ever be completely eliminated—requires that teachers recognize the strategy and then find a way to eliminate the payoff for using that strategy.

5
chapter

Communication

Human beings are social animals. From our first moments, we are immersed in an environment of verbal and nonverbal interaction. The relationship between teacher and student, parent and child, is mediated by verbal and nonverbal communication. Changing a relationship with a child starts with changing the language we use.

Lack of Awareness. We think we know what we're saying and how we sound, but often we don't. Every semester for the last three years, I have asked teachers, parents, counselors, and administrators in my classes to make tape recordings of themselves interacting with another person in a conflict situation and then to transcribe the tape. Over and over, the reaction to the tapes is one of surprise: "Did I say that?" "Do I sound like that?"

Those who have made a tape and listened to it are often embarrassed and are reluctant to say anything about their experience. They don't want to admit to not being the model teacher or parent—especially not in front of other teachers and parents. Some feel guilty that they didn't do a better job resolving the conflict situation they recorded.

Communication Based on Cultural Models. As children, we learn to "talk like a parent" from our parents. As a student, we learn to "talk like a teacher" from our teachers. We tend to fall into certain stereotyped patterns of behavior that we can recognize (when listening to others) as sounding like a parent or sounding like a teacher. Other patterns we recognize as sounding like a spoiled child. These patterns are comprised of certain attitudes, language, and tones of voice. Helping an individual to realize that "I sound like my father (or mother)," or that "I sound like my teachers" can be enough of a stimulus that it can lead to finding other ways of talking.

THE LANGUAGE
OF DISCOURAGEMENT

Regardless of the words used, the language that discourages people from accepting responsibility for their behavior, from learning, from becoming competent, and from cooperating is language that attacks the individual's self-image, leading him or her to feel powerless. It may seem strange to suggest that we should be concerned with helping children to feel more powerful—especially in those situations where a child is already so powerful that he or she can't be controlled. People, both children and adults, who manipulate or even dominate their environment seldom feel that they have the power to control their own behavior. They have little or no idea that they can change what happens to them by changing their behavior.

The language teachers and parents commonly use to communicate with children attempts to control the child rather than to encourage him or her to assume responsibility for self. The most common ways this is done are through blaming, questioning, inducing guilt feelings, ordering, and giving advice. Gordon (1974) uses the term "roadblocks" to describe these approaches.

Blaming. Accusations and blaming do not encourage others to accept responsibility for their behavior. Just the opposite. Accusation and blaming are directed at the person, not at the deed.

Questioning. Few responses could be more calculated to cut off communication than asking a barrage of questions; yet many people feel that they must ask questions in order to keep a conversation going. Questions tend to put the other person on the defensive, especially if a sensitive topic is being discussed.

Inducing Guilt. All forms of guilt induction tend to close off conversation. Combining guilt induction with questioning is a particularly effective way of putting others on the defensive.

Ordering and Giving Advice. In a conflict situation, ordering is generally useless. Giving advice is usually a form of gentle order: "Do this" is phrased as "Why don't you do this?"

"You" Statements. The word that is used most often to communicate nonacceptance and that cuts off communication is the word "you." This word and the tone of voice in which it is said is often used to put the other person on the defensive, as in the following statements:

- You don't do anything right!" (Accusation).
- "It's your fault" (Blaming).
- "You should be ashamed of yourself" (Inducing guilt feelings).
- "You better shape up" (Ordering).
- "You ought to get this done" (Advising).

There are dozens of variations, although the important thing is the tone of voice used. It is difficult to indicate a tone of voice in print. Most of the meaning in these phrases comes from the tone of voice. It is difficult to say any of the above phrases (or their dozens of variations) without making them sound like an attack.

Not Listening. When we fall into stereotyped responses, the language seems to take over. We find ourselves saying things our teachers and parents said to us. We seem to be running through a tape recording. When we're running through one of these tape recordings, we're not listening. The other person feels that he or she is not understood. The complaints that are probably most common from children and teenagers are, "You don't understand," and "You don't listen." These complaints are probably justified in most cases. What they mean is not simply that adults don't hear the words (which happens often enough) but that adults don't listen and accept their viewpoint. It's hard to realize that we do this because we think of ourselves as listening, and we aren't aware that we aren't listening.

When we use "you" statements, we're not listening. When we're blaming, questioning, inducing guilt feelings, ordering, or giving advice, we're not listening. Instead, we're concentrating on what *we* have to say, and it is impossible to listen to another person and be thinking about what we are going to say at the same time.

Listening Doesn't Mean Hearing the Words. Listening means being aware of the point of view of the other person. We easily respond as if the other person's view is the same as our own. Here are some common responses that deny the existence and/or validity of the other person's point of view:

SPEAKER: I'm really upset about my grade."

LISTENER: "You should have studied harder" (Blaming).
            "Why didn't you study harder?" (Questioning).

"You deserve to feel upset" (Inducing guilt).

"You better study harder next time" (Ordering).

"Why don't you set up a regular study time?" (Advising).

All of these responses indicate that the listener wasn't listening because they all ignore the speaker's feeling of being upset. Instead, the listener changes the subject to reforming the speaker.

Listening Means Staying with the Listener's Agenda. When we're concerned with what we have to say, we stop listening and change the agenda from what the speaker wanted to talk about to what we want to talk about. The change can be blatant or subtle, but the change leaves the speaker feeling that we aren't really listening. This is what kids mean when they say, "You never listen."

Examining Dialogue. Everything that has been said so far comes down to little more than good general advice. Awareness and change can come about only by examining one's own language. Examining the dialogue of others, however, is useful to understanding one's own interactions, provided that this does not become a substitute for looking at our own language.

The following dialogue took place between an elementary-school teacher and one of her students, Daphney.

TEACHER: Daphney, do you remember that you asked me to move Nicole from your—ah—from sitting next to you? Ah. . .why—why did, why did you want me to do that? [Daphney had asked the teacher previously to move her seat and the teacher is trying to resolve the conflict.]

DAPHNEY: 'Cause she kept on talking to me.

TEACHER: And you're a very bright little girl, and a very smart little girl [false praise], and you love to do what the teacher asks you to do [inducing guilt]. So, is it — is it that you don't want anyone talking — ah — that talks sitting next to you?"

DAPHNEY: Yes, ma'am.

TEACHER: Well, that's a very wonderful quality [false praise]. However, since you're such a nice little girl and such a bright little student [false praise, condescension], I believe you could probably help Nicole by setting a good example for her [giving advice]. If she stays — if she remains sitting next to you, don't you think that probably she would stop all of that talking and would really behave herself? [questioning, advising].

DAPHNEY: Yes, ma'am.

TEACHER: Therefore, Daphney, would you be willing for Nicole to remain sitting next to you?" [Teacher's solution ignores Daphney's request completely.]

DAPHNEY: Yes, ma'am.

TEACHER: Well, that's just fine — ah — and I thank you very much, Daphney. Do you have anything else to say, Daphney?

DAPHNEY: No, ma'am.

TEACHER: All right, thank you.

The dialogue sounds almost like a parody, although it is not. The teacher has done almost all of the talking, and she assumes all the way through that the child takes her viewpoint. On the positive side, the teacher does not blame or accuse Daphney; she doesn't humiliate the student but, instead, relies on persuasion. This is an important point, because far from being sadistic or mean, this teacher is doing her best to do a good job. She was well aware that she was making a tape, and it seems reasonable to assume that she wanted to put herself in the best light she could.

Although I am critical of what the teacher says in this dialogue, I admire her for her honesty in reporting what actually was on her tape recording and for her willingness to analyze what had happened. The teacher writes the following:

> In this particular situation, I am afraid that I was manipulating Daphney in order to arrive at the outcome I desired rather than at the outcome she desired.

As so often happens, although the student agreed with the teacher, the problem was solved only for the moment.

> Actually, it did not solve the problem in the long run, because one or two days later, Daphney approached me again with the same problem — namely, to "please move her seat away from Nicole's seat."

The next dialogue consists mostly of questions. This dialogue is a transcript by a teacher of her conversation with one of her sixth-grade students:

TEACHER: I'm glad you came in on time this morning and this afternoon. This is the first day this week that you've been here on time in the morning and the afternoon. When I saw you here this morning, I thought we'd have a good day. But I don't think you did your assignments this morning. Am I correct? [The teacher attempts to start on a positive note, but actually she makes her praise into an accusation in the second sentence when she ways "This is the first day this week...."]

JIMMY: Yes.

TEACHER: Why not? Why not? [Questioning; inviting excuses].

JIMMY: I don't know.

TEACHER: Did you understand them? [The teacher begins a whole series of questions.]

JIMMY: Yes.

TEACHER: Did you understand the "Getting the Main Idea" that we did for reading? [Questioning].

JIMMY: Yes.

TEACHER: Did you have any trouble with the words? [Questioning].

JIMMY: No.

TEACHER: But you did not do the assignment. Why not? [Questioning].

JIMMY: (No answer).

TEACHER: Did you take the test Miss Anthony [the student teacher] gave in math? [Questioning].

JIMMY: Yes.

TEACHER: Did you do all of it? [Questioning].

JIMMY: Yes.

TEACHER: Do you think you got 100 or 90%? [Questioning].

JIMMY: I don't know.

TEACHER: Did you study for the test last night? [Questioning].

JIMMY: Yes.

TEACHER: Then you had a lot of trouble with the class this morning — hitting people, bothering them. What was the cause of that? [Questioning. The teacher has changed the subject for the second time instead of solving one problem at a time.]

JIMMY: Gloria and them kept on messing with me.

TEACHER: How were they messing with you? [Questioning].

JIMMY: Gloria kept on asking me questions.

TEACHER: How were they messing with you? [Teacher repeats the previous question.]

JIMMY: Gloria kept on asking me questions.

TEACHER: What kind of questions? [Questioning].

JIMMY: Gloria kept on asking me if I'm scared of Eduardo and stuff.

TEACHER: Why didn't you tell me Gloria was bothering you? [Questioning].

JIMMY: (No answer).

TEACHER: I asked you questions this morning and you just refused to talk to me. Why did you do that? Do you know why you did that? [Questioning. If the teacher had realized what she was doing, she would know why Jimmy doesn't talk to her.]

JIMMY: No.

TEACHER: You've done it before, and I can't help you if you don't talk to me. I think I'm giving you work that you understand. If I'm not, I have no way of knowing it if you don't do the work so I can see it. Can you tell me what I can do that will help you get your assignments done? Do you have any ideas? [Questioning, blaming].

JIMMY: No.

The conversation goes on in the teacher's transcript for another page and a half. Although the teacher is asking a lot of questions, she's not really getting any information. She's doing all the talking, and Jimmy gives mostly one-word answers. In her eagerness to solve Jimmy's problems, she tries to do too much and becomes frustrated. She's taking most of the responsibility for solving Jimmy's problems, which is not likely to encourage him to cooperate. Many people assume that asking questions is the only way to get information, but, as this dialogue shows, asking questions can easily succeed in cutting off the flow of information. Jimmy needs encouragement to talk about his problems and to accept responsibility for them. Listening is much more likely to be an effective way to find out what the problem is and what can be done about it.

LISTENING SKILLS

Once people become aware of roadblocks in their communication, the problem is learning what to do about it. Learning listening techniques can be extremely useful. The techniques that are discussed here are taught to counselors as part of their education. The best technique is to have none, to be free of any crutches. The techniques that follow are not ends in themselves; they are intended to help teachers become better listeners as well as to help teachers become aware of alternatives to using roadblocks.

Silence. Interested silence invites others to talk. Particularly when someone has something that he or she wishes to pour out without interruption, simply keeping silent will encourage communication. The communication is still a two-way communication because attentive silence conveys interest and concern.

Listening Noises. "Umhmm. . . ." "Yes. . . ." "Go on. . . ." "I see. . . ." These expressions, although they may be clichés, are useful in encouraging others to talk.

Nonverbal Expression. Maintaining eye contact lets the other person know that you're interested without your having to interrupt. Some people use a nod of the head to indicate that they understand what's being said.

Reflecting What Is Being Said. This is a technique developed by Carl Rogers, the father of client-centered therapy (1969, 1970). The technique consists of repeating key phrases or sentences. For example:

STUDENT: "I didn't finish my homework for today."

TEACHER: "You didn't finish your homework" [Matter-of-fact, nonaccusing tone of voice].

To some, this may sound like the teacher isn't saying anything, but several important things are being communicated:

1. The teacher is letting the student know that he or she is listening.
2. The teacher is putting the responsibility for what comes next on the student.
3. The teacher is inviting the student to continue.
4. The teacher is not going to put the student on the defensive by asking questions, demanding an explanation, blaming, or inducing guilt feelings.

Paraphrasing. It isn't necessary to repeat verbatim what someone has said in order to use the Rogers technique. Paraphrasing achieves the same objectives without sounding stilted, as sometimes happens when literal repetition is used.

STUDENT: "I didn't finish my homework for today."

TEACHER: "You look pretty upset."

STUDENT: "Yeah, I don't want to get an "F" on it."

Summarizing. It isn't necessary or even desirable to repeat or paraphrase every sentence. Typically, when the other person has a lot to say, it is sufficient to summarize what's been said every so often. Several examples follow:

- A student has just finished describing an upsetting incident at home. The teacher says, "So you're pretty upset about what happened."
- A child has just finished describing a field trip at school that she feels excited about. The parent says, "You had a really exciting time!"

Why Listening Skills Are Effective. The listening skills discussed are effective in producing the following results:

1. Provide feedback to the speaker, letting him or her know that the other person is listening.
2. Encourage the speaker to talk.
3. Help the listener to be a better listener.
4. Provide information to the listener that would be difficult to get otherwise. (You will learn much more about students by listening than by asking questions; they will volunteer information you wouldn't otherwise get.)
5. Allow the listener to listen without interfering, blaming, offering advice, inducing guilt feeling, or throwing up roadblocks.

Roadblocks and Listening. Becoming aware of communication roadblocks is often not sufficient for change. Practicing listening skills is an effective way to stop throwing out roadblocks. Reflecting and summarizing what the other person is saying is an effective way to avoid questioning. It gives the listener something to do that is not a roadblock.

The following comments are by a woman who recognized the

need to change her behavior and who found that actively practicing these skills helped her to avoid roadblocks. At the time she took the class in which this report was written, she was not teaching (it was summer), but she found that she could apply the skills in her marriage:

> During the last few months, I've realized that I have the horrible habit of second-guessing and interrupting other people during conversations. This especially upsets me because they are two of the things that most infuriate me in other people. Not long ago, my husband was trying to tell me about what his day at work had been like. Every fourth word, there I was, finishing sentences (incorrectly, by the way), guessing outcomes, and interrupting — until he gave up and became quiet. I realized this too late and resolved to behave differently next time.

> The next time he began to talk about work, I made a point of looking directly at him while he talked, rephrasing bits of what he was saying to let him know that I had heard him and to help me remember it. (I remember with embarrassment the time that he had just finished about ten sentences, of which I did not hear *one*, and then I asked him about what he had just told me.) By listening, I enabled myself to give my husband my full attention, and I know by the way he acted and talked that he appreciated it. I learned a little more about him and grew up a little. I'm trying to practice this more and more, and I can tell the difference it's making — he's talking a lot more and sharing more things with me.

As the woman who wrote this indicates, she was aware of the problem before she knew what to do about it. She also indicates that she was not very patient with herself when she talks about finishing other people's sentences and interrupting ("two of the things that infuriate me about other people"). Having good intentions to change didn't help. When she found something she could practice doing ("rephrasing bits of what he was saying"), she had something to do instead of finishing sentences or interrupting.

THE LANGUAGE
OF ASSERTIVENESS

In a problem situation where a teacher or parent has needs that are not being met, listening is not enough. Listening by itself is useful in helping the other person to meet his or her needs, but it will not be sufficient in resolving the listener's unmet needs. It is essential for people who want their own needs met to ask for what they want. Not asking for what you want can easily lead to permissiveness. On the other hand, demanding what you want, laying down the law, or ordering what you want easily leads to aggressive, authoritarian behavior.

Assertiveness, as used here, refers to the honest expression of thoughts and feelings, not to a method of getting your own way:

Using the Word "I." Asking for what you want, expressing thoughts, or sharing feelings is more direct and effective when you use the word "I" in a direct statement: "I want. . .," "I would like. . .," "I don't like. . .," "I feel. . .," and so on.

The word "I" doesn't always make an "I" sentence. The term *"I" sentence* as used in this chapter refers to sentences where the speaker speaks about self. Sticking the words "I think," "I feel," or "I believe" in front of a "you" sentence, in front of a factual statement, or in front of a generality, does not make an "I" sentence in the sense in which it is used here. There is little or no difference in the following sentences:

- "Students don't show enough respect to teachers these days."
- "I think students don't show enough respect to teachers these days."

Both statements are essentially the same; both statements are generalities.

From General to Specific Statements. Using the word "I" requires a speaker to become very specific. One of the ways people avoid responsibility for their statements is to speak in generalities. Using the word "I" requires the speaker to find a specific verb in order to complete the sentence. When class discussions start to become too theoretical and abstract, I ask for "I" statements. For example, a statement such as "Students don't show enough respect to teachers" is a glittering generality I have heard over and over. Asking someone who has just said that sentence to make it into an "I" sentence requires that the speaker make his or her own specific complaint. The sentence might become one of the following: "I don't know what to do when students sass me," "I don't like it when I'm not given the respect I think I deserve," or, "I was more respectful of my teachers than many students are of me." The possibilities are infinite.

From Pseudo-Truth to Responsibility. Using an "I" sentence is a way of accepting responsibility for what is being said. Let's look at two sentences—one indirect, in which the speaker assumes no responsibility, and the second one direct, in which the speaker puts him- or herself on the line:

- Indirect: No one likes this rule.
- Direct: I don't like this rule.

Another example:

- Indirect: You shouldn't interrupt me.
- Direct: Excuse me, I don't like it when you interrupt.

The direct statements are much more powerful because they establish problem ownership. In the direct statements, the speaker accepts responsibility for his or her own feelings. In the indirect statements, the speaker puts the responsibility on someone else.

From Invulnerability to Vulnerability. People avoid "I" sentences because "I" sentences make them vulnerable. Willingness to make oneself vulnerable, however, is essential in establishing an effective working and helping relationship with others.

Using "I" is important in validating others by telling them our positive feelings towards them. Children who want validation from their parents often have a hard time getting it, especially in families where parents did not receive validation from their own parents. It is difficult for many parents to understand the difference between saying "You did a good job" and "I appreciate what you did."

From Nonassertive to Assertive. Nonassertive statements are indirect. We hope that the other person will understand what we want without having to ask for it. We avoid the risk of being turned down directly, but we are also likely to be turned down much more often. "I" sentences are assertive when we say what we mean. Indirect statements that beat around the bush are much more likely to be ineffective.

Many people are afraid to say what they mean because they're afraid of being refused or even rejected. By being indirect, however, they make it easier for others to misunderstand, to turn them down, or to reject them without even realizing it.

From Aggressive to Assertive. The communication roadblocks we have discussed, especially those using "you" sentences, tend to be aggressive. Using "I" sentences allows one to change aggressive statements to assertive ones:

- Aggressive: "You're late again. Why can't you be on time?"
- Assertive: "I feel upset when you're late because I have to wait, and I don't like waiting."

The second statement is a powerful statement, and it may even provoke some defensiveness. On the other hand, it is much more likely to be effective, because the speaker owns a problem and stays focused on that problem instead of attacking the other person.

Confrontation: Gordon's Three-Part "I" Message. The three-part "I" message developed by Dr. Thomas Gordon (1974) is an effective way of handling confrontations in problem situations. Gordon's "I" message consists of three parts: (1) a statement of the specific behavior that is causing a problem; (2) a statement of how the speaker feels about the situation; and (3) a statement of the specific, concrete effect the problem behavior is having on the speaker. Here's an example:

> "When you come to class late [statement of the problem-causing behavior], I feel frustrated [statement of the speaker's feelings] because I have to interrupt my lecture until you are settled" [statement of the specific effect the problem behavior has on the speaker].

Inappropriate Use of "I." The word "I" can be very effective when it is used to own a problem, to express appreciation, to validate others, or to share a feeling. The word "I" is inappropriate when it's not needed or when it's used to establish an authoritarian relationship. For examples, look at the following:

- It's unnecessary and inappropriate to preface ideas, observations, or statements of fact with "I think," "In my opinion," "I believe," or other such phrases, especially when teaching. There may be times when it is appropriate to use these phrases when giving a personal belief, but it becomes distracting when you're teaching a subject to qualify your statements constantly.

- It's unnecessary and inappropriate to use "I" to talk about oneself; rather, it's not so much the use of "I" but the talking about oneself that is inappropriate. This point is regularly made by teachers in my classes when the whole subject of "I" sentences is brought up. We are raised to think that using "I" is egotistical, and therefore, that it should be avoided. In fact, there are people who are obnoxious because they talk about themselves and seem to be using the word "I" constantly.

- It's unnecessary and inappropriate to use "I" in giving directions or instructions. "I want you to get in line" is much more likely to provoke resistance and resentment than a polite, "Please get in line." Using "I" to give orders sounds authoritarian, and it emphasizes the authority figure rather than the desired action. "Please turn to page such-and-such" is much more direct and appropriate than "I want you to turn to page such-and-such."

COMBINING LISTENING AND ASSERTIVENESS SKILLS

Many problems can be solved using a combination of listening and assertiveness. Listening is essential because it puts the other person — whether child or adult — on an equal footing. The act of listening is itself an act of encouragement. By listening, we make the other person a partner in the problem-solving process. Assertiveness is essential because it encourages the other person to listen to us and our needs.

There are times when another's behavior cannot be ignored by a teacher. When this happens, the teacher has a problem. The student may be the cause of the problem, but it's the teacher's problem, because the teacher has to deal with the behavior. An effective way of dealing with such a problem is to confront the student honestly and directly without beating around the bush but without throwing out roadblocks.

An effective sequence is to begin with an assertive statement, to listen to the other person's side, and then, if necessary, to reiterate your own concerns. The following example is a composite dialogue based on role-plays and taped dialogues:

Situation: The teacher is concerned about a failing student who is hostile toward the teacher.

TEACHER: Jane, I'm really concerned about your grades in this class since you haven't taken the last two tests. ["I" statement. Teacher expresses concern without blaming. Teacher is confronting student in an assertive way.]

STUDENT: It's not *your* problem. I'm the one getting the grade. [Student feels defensive and reacts by being aggressive.]

TEACHER: You're right, it is your problem, but I'm still concerned. I'd like to see you pass the course. [Ignores aggressive behavior of student; establishes problem ownership; uses "I" statement to express concern.]

STUDENT: No matter what I do in here now, I'm going to fail. So what's the use? [Student is discouraged; feels powerless to do anything.]

TEACHER: You're pretty discouraged about the class [reflecting feelings]. It seems to you like there's nothing you can do to pass [reflecting content].

STUDENT: I feel like it's no use.

TEACHER: Umhmm [listening noises].

STUDENT: I'd like to take a retest. I know you said you didn't want to give retests.

TEACHER: That's true. I don't like to give retests. I *would* be willing to make an exception. [Teacher says what he is willing to do.]

STUDENT: Could I take a retest next Monday during class?

TEACHER: I'd be willing to give a retest during one of my free periods next week. [Teacher says what he is willing to do.]

STUDENT: I can't come then.

TEACHER: I see. [Silence.] [Teacher waits for student to propose another solution.]

STUDENT: I could come after school, but I don't want to because of my job.

TEACHER: It sounds like we have a problem. [Teacher shares responsibility for the problem. Summarizes situation.]

STUDENT: I guess I could come after school.

TEACHER: I'd be willing to do that.

STUDENT: O.K.

In this situation, the teacher was concerned, but the problem was really the student's. If the student hadn't decided to cooperate, there would have been no solution. The teacher used "I" statements to say how he felt and what he was willing to do without blaming or lecturing the student. The teacher refused to be provoked by the student's initial hostile reaction, realizing that the student's feelings were *her* problem. The teacher did not "get on her case," nor was he a pushover.

What if the student didn't show up at the time agreed upon? The problem might be solved another way, or it might remain unresolved. It's not always possible to solve every problem. The teacher, however, could continue to use his listening and assertive skills with the student. Some teachers feel that a technique is not successful if a problem is not solved in the way they would like it to be. The purpose of these techniques, however, is to keep communication open. Teachers and students can be successful in doing this even if a problem is not solved. Keeping communication open keeps the possibility of solving problems in the future alive.

Solving Solvable Problems. Listening and assertiveness skills are effective in solving problems that *can* be solved. They cannot solve problems that cannot be solved. Put in this form, the statement is a circular proposition and doesn't say a thing. We need to remind ourselves, however, that we can't solve all problems, no matter what we do.

Let's look at another situation, that of cheating. In this dialogue, the teacher uses her skills in order to confront a student without putting the student down or making the cheating a moral issue:

Situation: A teacher has noticed a student looking in the direction of another student's paper during the course of a test. The teacher is having a private conference with the student afterwards.

TEACHER: I'm not giving you credit for this test. ["I" statement. Teacher says what she is going to do. Avoids blaming.]

STUDENT: Why not?

TEACHER: I saw you looking around throughout the test. [Avoids accusation. Describes specific behavior she observed. Resists the temptation to say, "You know why."]

STUDENT: But I wasn't cheating! I just like to look out the window.

TEACHER: That's possible, but you were looking around a great deal, so I am not willing to give you credit for the test. You have the choice of taking an F or taking a retest. [Teacher says what she will do. Avoids accusation.]

STUDENT: But I wasn't cheating!

TEACHER: You're pretty upset about what happened [reflecting feelings].

STUDENT: Yes, I don't want my parents to find out because I'm already in trouble because of my report card.

TEACHER: Your parents have been pressuring you to do better [reflecting content].

STUDENT: They really got on me when I brought my report card home last week. They said if I didn't start doing better I wouldn't be able to watch TV or go out after school or anything.

TEACHER: You're pretty scared about what might happen [reflecting feelings].

STUDENT: Yeah...

TEACHER: You feel like you have to do well [summarizing].

STUDENT: Yes, if I get an F on this, I won't be able to do anything!

TEACHER: You can retake the test.

STUDENT: Do I have to? I really wasn't cheating! [Student tries one last time to get the teacher to let him off the hook.]

TEACHER: You can retake the test tomorrow if you want.

STUDENT: O.K. I guess I will.

Notice that the teacher sidestepped the whole question of whether the student was cheating. The student felt under pressure, and the teacher might reasonably conclude that both the cheating and the denial were attempts to deal with that pressure. What if, some might ask, the student really was just looking around? The way the teacher handled the situation would still have been appropriate. The teacher based her decision on unacceptable behavior by the student: looking around during a test. Whether he was actually cheating or not, the behavior of looking around was still unacceptable to the teacher.

SUMMARY

The usual methods of trying to change others often end up discouraging them. Blaming, accusing, inducing guilt feelings, giving advice, or ordering puts the other person on the defensive and shut off communication. These methods may work at times in the short run, but in the long run, they tend to make students feel powerless and discouraged.

Listening encourages the other person to talk, to accept responsibility, and to attempt problem solving. Using listening techniques can be effective in becoming a better listener. Silence and nonverbal encouragement, such as maintaining eye contact, are among the most effective techniques to encourage communication. The Rogerian techniques of reflecting what is being said, reflecting the other person's feelings, and summarizing, complement silence and nonverbal techniques.

Assertiveness is necessary when the teacher has unmet needs. By making "I" statements, by saying what is acceptable, and by focusing on what they will do or are willing to do, teachers can assert themselves without being either authoritarian or permissive.

Listening and assertive techniques are effective in solving problems, but even when their use does not result in a solution, they can still function to keep the lines of communication open as well as to maintain a positive relationship with the other person.

6
chapter

Dealing With Criticism*

Effective teaching involves giving feedback to students—correcting errors, solving problems, making suggestions for change. Such feedback often includes criticism—of a piece of work, an idea, a situation, or an action. Criticism, however, can become a negative personal attack rather than a constructive evaluation. Teachers, like other mortals, may criticize the person instead of the problem.

In order to take a good look at the way criticism is given and received, let's divide criticism into two categories: *image-centered* and *problem-centered*. The following discussion of constructive criticism is based on rational–emotive therapy, an approach to life

*A revision of "Dealing with Criticism." Martin, R.J. *Learning*, March 1979, 92-93.

developed by psychotherapist Albert Ellis (1957, 1975, 1977, 1978) and an approach to language created by Korzybsky (1933) and developed by Ellis and others. This approach emphasizes analyzing and changing the sentences people use to describe themselves and others.

IMAGE-CENTERED CRITICISM

Image-centered criticism attacks the image an individual has of him- or herself. It identifies an individual with a generally negative label, such as *irresponsible, irrational, stupid, superficial, incompetent, untalented, worthless, trivial, irrelevant, selfish, uncreative,* or *greedy.* The label, however, reveals the standards of the person or group making the criticism, not those of the person to whom the criticism is addressed. What does "irresponsible" mean? Actions that one person regards as irresponsible (getting a divorce, going on strike, voting for a maverick candidate, marrying the "wrong" person, letting the grass grow "too high"), others may regard as quite responsible.

Image-centered criticism attempts to identify a person with a judgment: "You are irresponsible" communicates the message that *you* and *irresponsibility* are permanently linked together. Such criticism conveys two contradictory messages: (1) You should and must change immediately, and (2) you are the way you are and can't change even if you want to. Image-centered self-criticism, such as "I am irresponsible," produces the same effect.

Such messages can produce frustration and discouragement. Being the target of image-centered criticism tends to leave a person feeling powerless ("I can't do any better") and guilty ("I should be able to do better"). This unproductive combination usually leads either to paralysis ("I can't do it") or to violent resistance (temper tantrums, fighting, arguing).

PROBLEM-CENTERED CRITICISM

Problem-centered criticism focuses on solving problems, including changing behavior, without threatening an individual's self-image. This kind of criticism attempts to identify specific situations, behaviors, or attitudes that can be changed. "You are irresponsible" communicates no useful, specific information. "You left the water running; will you turn it off?" or "You made a right turn instead of a left turn" provides specific information and focuses on an individual's responsibility without attacking his or her self-image. Problem-centered criticism can also be effectively applied to oneself. Discouraging image-centered self-criticism — such as "I guess I'm stupid" or "I'm a failure" — can be rephrased to concentrate on this immediate problem: "I made a wrong turn," "I'll do this over later," or "I failed this time."

Although we may intend to give problem-centered criticism, we sometimes end up giving image-centered criticism. For example, a teacher discussing an essay containing several spelling errors might mean to say, "There are six spelling errors in your paper; please correct them," but may actually remark, "Good grief! Can't you spell any better than this?" People who intend to give problem-centered criticism may feel hurt and confused when others react to their statements with anger or frustration. The criticis may not realize that they ended up giving image-centered criticism out of habit and without thinking.

Defensive Reactions to
Problem-Centered Criticism

Sometimes problem-centered criticism is interpreted as being image-centered. This occurs when criticism has not been invited and is not wanted, when it comes at a time of high ego involvement, or when it is interpreted in light of a history of discouragement and failure. At these times, the person being criticized feels defensive. For example, look at the following statements:

CRITICISM: "Your paper has too many adjectives. Try taking some out."

RESPONSE: "What do you mean, 'too many adjectives'? I think they're good. I went to a lot of trouble to put them in."

CRITICISM: "There are a lot of spelling errors in your paper."

RESPONSE: "I can't understand that. I'm really a good speller and try to be careful."

CRITICISM: "Several parents are upset about the new reading program and would like to talk with you."

RESPONSE: "What do they have to complain about? I put in a sixty-hour week trying to teach their children."

In each of these examples, the response to criticism is a defensive one.

STRATEGIES FOR ELIMINATING IMAGE-CENTERED CRITICISM

The Dilemma of Giving Criticism

Teachers and parents sometimes feel ambivalent about criticism, sensing that no matter what they do, it seldom turns out well. How many teachers have felt like this:

> Sometimes a situation comes up and I know I need to say something to a student, but I don't, because I don't want to deal with a hostile student — or worse — with a hostile parent. Other times, I want to say, "Look, don't you see what might happen?" Kids often have no idea about consequences, and you can't tell them. When I do start to say something in what I think is a reasonable way, it doesn't come out that way, and we both end up getting mad.

The following strategies can be useful in eliminating image-centered criticism without taking a permissive approach to problem situations.

Avoid Giving Criticism Unless It's Asked For. Many teachers find it difficult to avoid offering "helpful" criticism before it's wanted. If students don't ask for help, it may be because they are not ready to seek help. Sure, you are paid to teach, but how do you feel when someone starts giving you advice when you didn't ask for it? In many cases, the student already knows that he or she isn't doing well, and criticism, even when it is problem-centered, can be discouraging enough that it results in giving up rather than in improvement.

Rationally, it makes sense to avoid criticism when you notice that the criticism is not having a positive effect. We sometimes have trouble doing the rational thing, however, because we are told (most of the time we tell ourselves) that it is our job to keep after students and that we are not doing our job if we don't keep after the students. I remember watching my son, then in second grade, grow more and more discouraged about school because of difficulties in printing neatly (he is left-handed and has trouble holding a pencil). As the teacher's well-intentioned remarks on his papers continued to accumulate ("needs improvement," "try to do better," "try harder,"), he continued to grow more and more discouraged about school. Fortunately, the school year ended before he gave up completely.

It is essential to look at the effect criticism is having. If it is generating discouragement and giving up, it is not helping the student. The teacher who continued to offer "helpful comments" to my son did it because she thought that that is what good teachers do. We can all become easily trapped in this way. We give criticism (especially "constructive" criticism) because we feel that by doing so we are doing a good job, not because what we are doing is having a positive effect.

Help Others Cope with Their Own Image-Centered Self-Criticism. People who criticize themselves; put themselves down; or otherwise tell themselves that they are stupid, no good, bad, or worthless discourage themselves from acting more effectively. Children are particularly susceptible to self-criticism because they often experience criticism from parents and teachers. By encouraging children to avoid image-centered criticism of themselves, parents and teachers can help children concentrate on solving their problems. Use the strategies listed under "Strategies for Coping with

Image-Centered Criticism" to help students change their image-centered criticism to a problem-centered approach to their difficulties. Students who discourage themselves by telling themselves that they are stupid, no good, bad, or worthless will not usually respond to a problem-centered approach until they stop discouraging themselves.

Avoid Absolutes, Such as Always, Never, or Ever. Absolutes, such as *always*, *never*, or *ever*, imply image-centered criticism. Sentences such as 'You are *always* late," "Can't you *ever* get here on time?" or "You *never* help out" do not refer to a specific problem here and now. Such sentences don't state problems; they accuse and put down the guilty individual.

Be Specific. Refer to the specific problem at hand, no matter how many times it has happened before. If you want to punish the other person for being continually irresponsible, you can probably get him or her to feel bad by making general statements about his or her behavior, but you won't be solving the immediate problem.

Avoid the Verb "To Be." The language we use can trap us into vague, image-centered criticism. When we use any of the forms of the verb *to be* (am, is, are, was, were, have been, has been) in offering criticism, we easily fall into the trap of identifying the individual with his or her behavior. Image-centered criticism is invariably expressed with some form of the verb *to be*. By becoming aware of your sentences and then rephrasing them in order to eliminate the verb *to be*, more specific, problem-centered criticism will result. In order to avoid the verb *to be*, you will find that you are forced to make specific statements. A sentence such as "You are irresponsible" is an excellent example of image-centered criticism. It attacks without even mentioning a specific problem. The person criticized doesn't know what's wrong, what's upsetting the critic, or what could be done. By simply restating the criticism without the verb *to be*, the critic is forced to make the criticism more specific. For example, "You *are* irresponsible" might be changed to "You didn't clean up, and this creates a problem."

Listen to Your Tone of Voice. Few people are aware of their tone of voice when they give criticism. Tape-recording yourself can help you become more aware of what you say and how you say it. Tone of voice easily changes problem-centered criticism into image-centered criticism. An angry tone of voice is especially likely to be interpreted as directed at the individual rather than at the problem.

When Students Ask for Criticism, Find Out What They Want. Careful questioning may reveal that a request for criticism is actually an appeal for approval, an invitation to fight, a request for attention, or a genuine request for problem solving. There is little point in offering problem-centered criticism if the student is really looking for something else. Here are some examples of typical requests and what they *may* mean:

Situation: A student proudly holds up her painting and asks the teacher, "How do you like my painting?"

Interpretation: In the moment of creation, people like to feel good about what they've done; they're not usually interested in artistic criticism at that moment. After they have had time to enjoy their work, they may feel much more willing to have it evaluated. An appropriate response in this situation might be to use reflective listening: "You look like you feel proud of your painting," or, "You feel happy with your work!"

Situation: A student who feels upset at her grade comes up to the teacher and asks in an angry voice, "How come I got such a low grade?" The teacher has had conversations before with the student, and they usually end up fighting about the student's poor work.

Interpretation: If the student wants to get into a power struggle, the teacher is only cooperating by offering criticism. An appropriate answer to this student might be reflective listening focusing on the student's feelings: "You look pretty upset about your grade." Another response might be a friendly, "Let's talk about it," or, "Shall we talk about it?"

Avoid Using Criticism in Order to Try to Change Others. Image-centered criticism often results from an attempt to change a person by attacking self-image and by inducing guilt feelings. These methods of influencing others mistakenly attempt to bring about a change by trying to force others to change. Image-centered criticism is an attempt to coerce people to change. Conversely, attempting to coerce people to change usually results in image-centered criticism — and, of course, in little or no change.

STRATEGIES FOR COPING WITH IMAGE-CENTERED CRITICISM

Responding to criticism might seem to be a completely different problem from giving it, but the two problems are two sides of the same coin. Teachers often have the same reaction to criticism that students have. Coping more effectively with both giving and receiving criticism requires coming to grips with the patterns of language, beliefs, and emotions that make it difficult for us to change. Many teachers have felt like this at one time or another.

Sometimes, when someone criticizes me, I feel confused and don't know what to do. Sometimes I get angry — like when I've been bending over backwards to give a student a break, and then the student — or a parent — has the nerve to criticize me for not doing enough, or not doing it right, or whatever. Sometimes I just feel helpless — I don't know what to say. When my administrator came in to say that he'd been hearing complaints about me, I was speechless; I didn't know what he was talking about, so how could I respond? Sometimes, I go in the other direction. A student or a parent comes in and makes a critical remark, and I start explaining, reasoning, and defending what we're doing and why. That often makes the student or parent defensive, so even if I've won, I haven't really gained anything because they are not satisfied.

The following strategies are aimed at helping you to cope with image-centered criticism:

Question the Standards of Your Critic: Are They Your Own? Remember that image-centered criticism is simply an evaluation of an individual in terms of the critic's standards. People tend to be most affected by criticism that threatens their real or imagined status in a group. Ask yourself, "Whose standards am I failing to meet?" "Do I accept these standards?" For example, "Do I accept the standards of my neighbor who doesn't think I'm a good parent because I don't live up to his expectations?" If you decide that you don't want to live up to those expectations, you'll find it easier to accept the judgment as an opinion and not to get upset about it.

Avoid Defending Yourself. A defensive reaction almost always leads to defensive feelings and behavior, and this, in turn, encourages additional criticism.

Use Negative Inquiry. When image-centered criticism is given, problem-centered criticism can be encouraged by using negative inquiry, a technique described by Manuel Smith in *When I say No, I Feel Guilty* (1979). For example, to the charge, "You're irresponsible," reply, in a sincere way, "What is it that I'm doing that's irresponsible?", or "How am I acting irresponsibly?" Such a response will usually result either in problem-centered criticism ("You didn't clean up the room") or in the end of the conversation, if the critic has nothing substantive to complain about.

Change Absolute Statements to Probabilistic Statements. Rephrase sweeping criticisms so that they become statements dealing with specific problems. For example, if you receive the criticism, "You *always* come late," respond, without sarcasm, "I've been late several times recently."

You can also apply this strategy to self-criticism. Both children and adults discourage themselves by using absolute statements when criticizing themselves: "I always fail," "I never do anything right," "I'm no good at math," "I'm a failure," and so on. Changing these statements to nonabsolute terms can be useful in coping with discouragement: "Sometimes I fail," "I didn't do this right," or "I sometimes feel like a failure."

Eliminate the Verb "To Be" from Self-Critical Statements. Substitute a more problem-centered verb. For example, instead of saying, "I'm a failure" (identification or self with a label), say, "I failed at this task," "I made a mistake," or "I did that incorrectly." Instead of saying, "I'm irresponsible," substitute, "I acted irresponsibly when I didn't call." Eliminating the verb *to be* from criticism requires the speaker to be specific about the problem instead of relying on a generalization.

Listen to How Something Is Being Said. No matter how problem-centered a criticism may sound to the critic, the message conveyed to you may differ depending on the context, the tone of voice, the relationship of the critic to you, your past experiences, and so on. Ask for more information if you're not sure whether the criticism made to you is problem-centered or image-centered.

Treat All Criticism as Problem-Centered. When we respond to image-centered criticism by feeling defensive, hurt, or threatened, we are letting our critic get to us. We are probably irrationally telling ourselves that we have to defend ourselves. The alternative is to interpret all criticism as problem-centered. This is difficult, though by no means impossible. In fact, we all do it at times. For example, when a two-year-old tells me that I'm stupid, I don't get upset because I know that he or she is upset, and that I have no reason to feel threatened.

Interpreting image-centered criticism as if it were problem-centered is desirable because it allows the individual being criticized to judge the validity of the criticism without feeling defensive. The receiver accepts the image-centered criticism as information that can be used to make decisions rather than as a threat. For example, look at the following statements:

Criticism: "Is this the best you can do? Look at all the mistakes you've made!"

Response: "Thanks for telling me. I wasn't aware that there were so many."

Criticism: "You're the worst player I know; I can't play with you."

Response: "If that's how you feel, then you're probably right — we shouldn't continue to play."

Criticism: "You're a terrible parent. You never let me do the things Sammy's parents let him do."

Response: "It's true that I won't let you do all the things you want to do."

In each of these situations, the person being criticized refuses to take the criticism personally. Most people, however, including teachers, find this more easily said than done.

SUMMARY

Image-centered criticism attacks the person, often resulting in discouragement, resentment, and little or no change. Problem-centered criticism, by focusing on specific behavior or on situations that can be changed, encourages people to accept responsibility for solving problems.

Teachers know, in a general way, that image-centered criticism is not effective, but many do not know specific steps they can take to eliminate their own image-centered criticism. Eliminating the verb *to be* from criticism helps the critic to state criticisms in specific terms and to concentrate on situations and behavior rather than on personalities. Eliminating absolutes, such as *always, never,* and *ever,* will also lead to more specific, problem-centered criticism.

Teachers who find themselves objects of criticism (including self-criticism) can learn to treat all criticism as problem-centered, focusing on the problem rather than on themselves.

7
chapter

Coping
With Excuses *

Unacceptable behavior is an obvious discipline problem, but how do you deal with excuses? Accept them? Throw up your hands? Get angry? Teachers are sometimes not sure how to react; in part, this is because excuses are a culturally acceptable way of making amends or of avoiding a confrontation. When excuses become a means of avoiding responsibility or consequences, teachers face a problem.

*A revision of "Coping With Excuses." Martin, R.J. *Learning*, in press.

RECOGNIZING EXCUSES

Because excuse making is part of a deeply embedded cultural pattern we usually take for granted, recognizing an excuse is not always easy. We're conditioned to encourage excuse making by asking for reasons and explanations. A teacher friend put it this way: "Many times I was manipulated because I focused on the excuse instead of the behavior." She continued, "What the teacher is really after is a change in unacceptable behavior, and excuses will not aid in that change." We are lured away from focusing on the problem because we are trying so hard to be fair, or reasonable, or understanding, and we don't recognize that the student has avoided dealing with the consequences of an action.

What makes a statement an excuse is that it helps us to avoid responsibility for our actions. Here are six of the more common examples of excuses used by students and teachers alike:

Denial. It's easier to deny responsibility than to accept blame and guilt. "I didn't do it" is a typical response of students when confronted by teachers. Even when the statement is true, however, an individual may be partly responsible for what happened.

Blaming Others. People easily blame others or their environment for their own behavior. Examples: "The milk spilled. . . ." "Look what you made me do. . . ." "The glass fell off the table. . . ." "It's her fault. . . ."

Appeals to Circumstance. "I had to. . . ," "I had no choice. . . ," and "You force me to. . ." are excuses used more by adults than by children. By using such expressions, we avoid responsibility for our own decisions, and we also teach students to avoid responsibility for their decisions.

Appeals to Authority. Appealing to authority is similar to appealing to circumstances: "It's a rule," "It's traditional," "It's policy," or, "That's just the way it's done around here." When adults hide behind phrases such as these, students are encouraged to imitate them.

Somebody Who Is Not Really Me. Blaming oneself would seem to be identical to accepting responsibility, but people often blame themselves in a way that avoids responsibility: "That's just not like me," "I just don't know what came over me," or, "I couldn't help it." Such expressions excuse behavior by claiming that a behavior was beyond the individual's control.

Life Story. Personal history certainly influences us, but too often that history is used in order to avoid responsibility for present behavior. "I was just born this way," or, "I've never been any good at math": Such expressions create a self-fulfilling prophecy; they're a way of programming oneself.

BEHAVIOR TO AVOID

There are no magic formulas that will completely eliminate excuses. The suggestions that follow have two functions: (1) They avoid encouraging students to make excuses, and (2) they make excuses useless as a way of avoiding responsibility or consequences.

Don't Ask "Why?" When students do something they're not supposed to do, our immediate impulse is to ask, "Why did you do that?" First, students often don't know why they misbehave, why they don't have their assignments done, or why they forgot their books, so we are unlikely to find out much by asking. Second, asking "Why?" encourages excuse making or other defensive behavior unrelated to dealing with the problem. Students may learn to think up good explanations, but they won't learn to cope with the consequences of their behavior.

Don't Induce Guilt Feelings. Inducing guilt feelings is of no use in changing behavior and, in fact, makes change more difficult by convincing students that they are "bad." Guilt feelings reinforce a negative self-image and serve as an excuse for not changing (Dreikurs, 1967).

Avoid Discussions of Right and Wrong. Regardless of age, students know what is considered right and wrong. "Discussions" by adults of right and wrong tend to lecture, nag, and preach to the child about what he already knows. Such discussions only serve to humiliate and put down a student while establishing the moral superiority of the adult.

Avoid Moralizing. When students do give excuses, avoid the temptation to moralize. It is seldom necessary to talk with students about what they *should* do. They already know what they should do; they just don't want to do it. Moralizing only adds a layer of moral judgment to problems, making them more difficult to resolve. Moralizing focuses on making people feel bad about themselves, creating defensiveness and hostility. Moralizing encourages additional excuses rather than change and emphasizes the power of authority, minimizing the power and responsibility of the individual to control his or her own behavior. Finally, moralizing tends to focus on what *should* have happened instead of focusing on the problem — that is, what *did* happen and what can be done about it.

Discourage Good Intentions. Good intentions are promises we don't really intend to keep. "I should. . . ," "I'll try. . .," or, "I'll have to be more careful. . .": These expressions are actually excuses made in advance of failure. When someone uses these expressions, you can be reasonably sure that he or she will not follow through. Good intentions are not an expression of responsibility but an avoidance of it. By saying "I should. . . ," we substitute a statement of intent for a decision to take specific action.

Discount Good Intentions. Expressions of good intentions, no matter how sincere they seem, are a substitute for action. People easily use their seemingly sincere good intentions to avoid a confrontation. It's not that they're trying to fool others but rather that they succeed in fooling themselves. Students who express good intentions may sincerely intend to follow through on them, but they are unlikely to do so. Good intentions are like New Year's resolutions: Through experience, we learn that no matter how sincere we may feel, we are unlikely to carry through on them.

Like the rest of us, students often express good intentions because they are expected to do so. They express good intentions because they want to please and because they want to stay in the good graces of teachers and parents.

POSITIVE STEPS

The goal we're concerned with here is not to eliminate all explanations by students of their behavior but to make it clear that an explanation, no matter how truthful or accurate, does not entitle them to avoid responsibility for their actions.

"What Did You Do?" How many times have you been confronted with a barrage of excuses and have had trouble finding out exactly what had happened? One approach, reality therapy (developed by William Glasser, 1965), concentrates on asking everyone to state what he or she actually did. For example, when a student reports what others have done ("He started it"), listen politely and then ask, "What did you do?" You're not asking for reasons, excuses, or justifications—just for a simple statement of what happened.

Focus on the Present. When excuses are offered, listen politely, but focus on what can be done now: "What could you do about that?" "What do you want to do about it?" "What are you going to do about it?" Questions such as these, when asked in a nonjudgmental way, place the responsibility for the student's behavior back on the student. Such questions neither affirm nor deny the validity of an excuse. Instead, these questions sidestep arguments about excuses and focus on the present. "I forgot," or "The dog chewed up my paper" may be true statements about why a certain child doesn't have a homework paper, but why get trapped into accepting the situation as *your* problem (and then getting mad or frustrated)? By asking students to come up with solutions and to follow through on them, teachers can encourage students to be careful, to plan ahead, and to accept responsibility.

COMMUNICATION SKILLS

Putting it all together into an approach that works requires both assertiveness and good listening skills. Here's an example:

TEACHER: I see you boys have been fighting [not said as an accusation].

JAY: He started it [blaming others].

TEACHER: What did you do? [focus on Jay's behavior].

JAY: I hit him back [blaming others].

TEACHER: You hit Zeke [uses reflective listening; ignores excuse].

JAY: Yes, but he started it [blaming others].

TEACHER: [Ignoring Jay] Zeke, what did you do?

ZEKE: He called me a name, so I punched him [blaming others].

TEACHER: You punched Jay [uses reflective listening; ignores excuse].

ZEKE: He made me. If he hadn't called me a name, I wouldn't have punched him [blaming others; avoiding responsibility].

TEACHER: Yes.

This is only the first stage in the teacher's approach. The teacher may not sound very successful, but children don't always readily admit what they've done. Students who are used to being jumped on, criticized, punished, humiliated, or made to feel guilty often have trouble verbalizing what they did, even when they know you saw them do it. However, when you use Glasser's approach consistently, students begin to realize that you're not trying to pin blame on them but that you are concerned with solving a problem. They will become more willing to verbalize responsibility for their actions when they notice that you aren't treating them the way they expected. Don't expect this to work immediately with your biggest problems. I counseled a fifth-grade boy who was a severe behavior problem, and it was four months before I heard him describe a single incident in which he had gotten himself into trouble.

What comes next in this scene between Teacher, Jay, and Zeke is an attempt by Teacher to get the boys to propose a solution:

TEACHER: Well, what else could you do, Zeke, when someone calls you a name? [focusing on the problem behavior].

ZEKE: I could hit him [testing the teacher].

TEACHER: Yes, but what else could you do? [stays with the problem].

ZEKE: Tell the teacher? [hunting for the answer the teacher seems to want].

TEACHER: Yes, that's possible. You don't sound like you think that's a good solution.

ZEKE: I could just not punch him [good intentions].

TEACHER: Yes, that's a good idea, but I think you need to come up with something positive you can *do* to keep yourself under control.

ZEKE: I could walk away.

TEACHER: O.K. You want to do that next time, and we'll see how it works. Jay, what about you? What could you do instead of calling Zeke names?

JAY: Tell him I don't like it when he plays too rough.

TEACHER: O. K. Let's see how it goes.

The first question a teacher might ask about this dialogue is whether it's realistic and whether it will really solve the problem. I think that it is a realistic situation because there's a good chance that it won't solve the problem and that it will be necessary for the teacher to go back and try again! But if it is necessary for the teacher to try again, it doesn't mean that either the teacher failed or the approach failed. What makes this a realistic approach is that it does allow you to go back again and again and work on a problem. What brings results is the willingness to persist day in and day out.

At the same time, it is important to point out that, in many cases, the approach described here will be successful the first time, especially with students who really want to cooperate and be responsible but who have not been taught how.

SUMMARY

Making excuses is often a way of manipulating the environment in order to avoid consequences. When students become adept at avoiding the consequences of their behavior, they find it difficult to accept responsibility. By ignoring excuses and focusing on present behavior and what can be done about it, teachers can sidestep many power struggles while encouraging students to accept responsibility for their own behavior.

8
chapter

Encouraging Responsibility

What happens when a teacher leaves the classroom momentarily? Which students can you trust? How do you get students to follow through on a task? What do you do about excuses? All these questions are concerned with responsibility.

We use the word *responsible* in quite different, even contradictory ways. *Responsible* often means simply doing what you're told. We accuse students who don't follow rules, who don't do what they're told, and who don't do what we expect of being "irresponsible." The other common meanings we give "responsible" have more to do with choosing the best course of action in a particular situation, with acting out of concern for others, with using good sense, and with acting according to personal values.

There are two areas where students need encouragement to accept responsibility: first, responsibility for social behavior, especially in problem areas, and second, responsibility for learning.

PROBLEM OWNERSHIP

At the end of the course I teach each semester on teaching and parenting, I ask what has been most valuable. One of the most frequent answers voices a sense of relief and encouragement from realizing that teachers are not responsible for everything their students do. One aspect of learning to encourage responsibility in others is what Gordon (1974) calls "problem ownership." Gordon points out that teachers often have difficulty knowing whether a problem is theirs or the students'. When teachers try to solve problems that really belong to the students, they encourage irresponsible behavior. When teachers neglect problems that really belong to them, they encourage discipline problems.

When teachers feel responsible for solving problems that belong to others, they may find they have difficulty separating their own needs from the needs of others. Teachers find it hard to accept the mistakes and poor judgments of their students when they take responsibility for those mistakes. Why does this happen? In many cases, we get trapped into being guided by mistaken logic that goes something like this:

1. "Good teachers are responsible for solving all problems."
2. "If I can't solve this problem, I must not be a good teacher, and I will feel frustrated and guilty."
3. "I *have to* solve this problem."

This logic is not necessarily conscious. In fact, we may consciously reject this way of thinking, and yet we find ourselves feeling responsible, then trying to solve the problem, and finally feeling frustrated and angry if we don't succeed.

It's difficult for teachers to stop feeling responsible for solving problems that are not their own because they are constantly pressured to live up to an impossible ideal. Part of the pressure comes from teachers themselves. Part of the pressure comes from others, including parents, administrators, and students who have come to expect that teachers will take care of them. A teacher who refuses to accept responsibility for solving others' problems may be accused of not caring by other adults or even by the students themselves. When this happens, realize that students who avoid responsibility for their problems are not going to start accepting responsibility without a fight.

Teacher Problems. A teacher has a problem when a situation or behavior has a concrete, unacceptable effect on the teacher. It doesn't matter who is causing the problem; if it has an unacceptable effect on the teacher, it's the teacher's problem. For example, a teacher has a problem when:

- A student disrupts the class.
- One student punches another.
- A student is cheating, and the teacher catches him or her.
- A student interrupts the teacher.
- A student comes to class drunk.
- A student is smoking in school.
- A student writes on the wall.

In these situations, teachers need to take action. On the other hand, situations that may seem very similar to the examples above are really the student's problem:

- A student tells you she's been stealing.
- You know a student who's drinking and doing drugs on the weekend.
- A student is smoking off school property after school.
- A student comes late but is not disruptive.

A teacher may be very concerned about these problems, but they are not the teacher's problem.

The fact that you don't accept ownership for a student problem:

1. Does not mean that you don't care or aren't concerned.
2. Does not mean that you don't want to help.

A teacher may be very concerned and want very much to help, but there are important reasons why a teacher should not assume responsibility for a student's problems.

Why It's Important Not to Accept Responsibility for Others' Problems. Accepting responsibility for students' problems has these undesirable consequences:

1. Discourages students from accepting responsibility for own problems.
2. Makes it more difficult in the long run for students to cope with problems.
3. Leads to overprotectiveness.
4. Leads to nagging, moralizing, preaching, and other ineffective forms of coercion.

Positive Consequences of Not Accepting Responsibility for Others' Problems. Not accepting responsibility for others' problems has important positive consequences. Not owning the problems of others will result in the following:

1. Help you to keep your sanity. Counselors and psychiatrists quickly learn that they cannot accept responsibility for solving client problems. Those who do so can quickly become as depressed and suicidal as any of their clients.

2. Help you to listen better. When you don't feel that you have to solve the problem, you can listen better because you're not trying to solve the problem in your head while the student is talking.

3. Help you to be more empathetic. Empathy means understanding how another person feels and understanding their hurt, anger, and frustration without being hurt, angry, or frustrated ourselves. When we start feeling hurt, angry, or frustrated ourselves, we easily start moralizing, preaching, giving advice, or otherwise trying to bring about a solution by coercion.

4. Help to create a sense of understanding and mutual respect, even when no solution is forthcoming.

5. Encourage students to find out what they can do to solve their problems or, if the problems can't be solved, to find a rational way to cope with them.

Establishing in your mind who has the problem can also enhance your dealings with parents, administrators, spouse, and friends. Here are some situations where establishing problem ownership can be useful:

- A parent tells you she's unhappy with the school and how it's run.
- Your principal tells you she's upset with the way your class behaved with a substitute while you were in the hospital having an appendectomy.
- A student complains that your assignments are unfair.

In all three of these examples, the problem does not belong to the teacher. Simply thinking to oneself, "This is not my problem" is often sufficient to avoid accepting responsibility and its attendant defensive, frustrated, and angry feelings.

Problem Ownership: A Realistic Approach to Helping. Some readers may still be upset by the idea of not owning student problems, especially those that desperately need solutions. It is easy to make the irrational assumption that because we want desperately to help and because a solution is desperately needed, we can find a solution by owning this problem. Many teachers (and parents) mistakenly assume that if someone only cares desperately enough that a solution can and will be found. Television and the movies have encouraged this tendency to believe that we can create a happy ending if we just want it badly enough. Feeling desperate results in poor judgments more often than it succeeds in helping. Not owning others' problems is a more realistic approach to helping others than taking on their problems. We cannot always solve others' problems, no matter how much we want to. We can help others to solve or at least to cope with their problems by a willingness to listen and be supportive.

ENCOURAGING RESPONSIBILITY
FOR BEHAVIOR

Problem ownership presupposes responsibility for behavior. I can't be expected to solve my own problems if I'm not responsible for my behavior and if I'm not free to make decisions and then live with the consequences of those decisions.

"What Are You Going To Do About It?" William Glasser (1965) developed an approach to responsibility that is now called reality therapy. The basic idea of reality therapy, an idea originally developed by Adler's individual psychology (Adler, 1970; Ansbacher and Ansbacher, 1956) and Ellis's (1977) rational-emotive therapy, is that we are all — regardless of age, sex, ability, or past history — responsible for our own behavior and for what we do about problems. Glasser's approach to problem ownership is to ask, after a client has brought up a problem, "What are you going to do about it?" This question sidesteps any attempt by the client to put

responsibility on the counselor, and it also confronts the client with the question of what he or she can do. Asking this simple question is an effective way of putting everything that has been said so far about problem ownership into effect. The following example written by a sixth-grade teacher illustrates this technique as well as another technique developed by Glasser, that of asking the other person to make a value judgment about his behavior:

> I made a writing assignment and then gave the children time to work on it. Then I started to walk around the room to check on individual students. Immediately, Kevin was talking to his neighbors. He had barely written two sentences, and he had the urge to share them with his neighbors. I quietly walked over and asked him what he was doing. He answered that he was talking to his friends. Then I asked him if this was helping him complete his assignment. "No," he replied. I then asked him what we should do about it and what kind of plan he could come up with to deal with this situation. He thought briefly and decided that he could write quietly while finishing the project and that then he could be the first to share the written assignment with the class.

> Kevin did just that. He was very excited about his writing. I was pleased with his behavior and the quality of his written work. I think that Kevin felt more responsible for his own behavior since he had decided on the plan to correct it. If I had told him to do exactly what he was going to do to correct his behavior in no uncertain terms, he would not have felt a responsibility to correct the behavior.

In an authoritarian classroom, the teacher is responsible for keeping order, and so it is the teacher who fails if order is not kept. The teacher may have a good, orderly classroom, but the students do not feel that they have a stake in what happens. The teacher who wrote the above example adds the following:

> If Kevin had continued talking after he had decided on his plan of action, the burden of failure would have been on his shoulders. However, if I had decided on his plan and he had then disturbed his neighbors, I would have failed in the fact that I couldn't force him to change his behavior.

This teacher has caught on to the underlying principle of having good discipline: getting students to accept responsibility for their own behavior instead of trying to make them behave.

Many problems — perhaps the vast majority — that come up cannot be easily divided into teacher- or student-owned problems. The teacher who wrote about Kevin's accepting responsibility for his own behavior was careful to add the following:

> Sometimes, we teachers think that the problem is all in the hands of the student and that he or she must shape up and meet our needs or get out.

Getting students to accept responsibility for their behavior is often a matter of having a positive attitude and good listening skills, as the following report by a sixth-grade male teacher in an upper elementary school shows:

> Our school building is located one block from a "Dairy Sweet." When I first started teaching, the elementary kids could go over there for lunch if they brought a note. For numerous reasons, this practice ended about three years ago. Each year, when the Dairy Sweet opens, we have to go over the policy with our students. This year was no exception. I went over the policy last week, and no students had any questions. Then today, I had lunch duty with the fifth and sixth grades. I knew that two of my girls were not eating hot lunch, but I did not question it because I assumed that they had brought cold lunches. Then another teacher sat down beside me, and we began talking. She mentioned that one of her town students wanted to eat at the Dairy Sweet and that she had wanted two of my girls to go along. The teacher gave her student permission to go home but not to the Dairy Sweet. When she mentioned my two girls, I began to look for them.
>
> Since I have 110 students in the lunch room, I figured that they were somewhere in there. "No," someone said, "they went to the Dairy Sweet." So the other teacher walked to the Dairy Sweet and found the girls. She told them to report to me when they got back.

At this point the girls knew that they were in trouble. The teacher avoided moralizing or preaching and let the girls decide what should be done:

> When the girls came walking across the playground, I walked over to greet them. One said, "I guess we have some explaining to do," and I said, "I'm listening." They did not deny that they went to the Dairy Sweet, knowing it was against the rules.
>
> I praised them for telling me the truth. Then I asked them what they wanted to do to correct the situation. One suggested losing one day's recess since they had abused their recess privilege. The other decided that they should write a letter to their parents informing them that they had left the school grounds.

Many students, when asked what should be done, immediately resort to suggestions of punishment. It is important to help students to realize that punishment does not solve anything and that deciding what needs to be done means coming up with a positive plan instead of punishment. Staying in at recess sounds like punishment. Writing a letter to the parents explaining the situation seems like a much better plan because it relates directly to the situation at hand. What actually happened is that the teacher, rather than the students, ended up talking with the parents:

> The principal thought that I should call all of the parents and have all of my class sit together in the lunch room this week. All of the students involved are good students, and this was their first time in trouble. I was against calling the parents, but I did it. All of the parents were very understanding. They did not want their children sneaking away from school. I informed all of them that I was very pleased with all of the students for telling the truth and being sincere. I hope that these students will not do this again.

We don't know if the problem came up again. The real point of the example, however, is not that the girls didn't go back to the Dairy Sweet, but how the teacher handled the situation. An authoritarian approach relying on threats, moralizing, and preaching might have been just as effective in stopping the trips to the Dairy Sweet, but these methods tear down the student's self-concept and sense of responsibility rather than encouraging them.

ENCOURAGING RESPONSIBILITY
FOR LEARNING

The area of discipline and behavior problems is of concern to the teacher because misbehavior creates an obvious problem. Helping students to be responsible for their actions can be effective in solving behavior problems and creating an orderly classroom. This uses only a small part of the potential for encouraging responsibility. An orderly classroom is not an end in itself. Learning can take place best in a classroom where there isn't a constant battle between teacher and students. An orderly classroom in which students accept responsibility for their actions does not, however, ensure learning. Students must also feel encouraged to learn. Encouragement to learn doesn't come from praise (although this may be helpful at times); from stimulating materials (although these are important); or from an interested, energetic teacher (although interest and energy in a teacher are essential); but from the students themselves. Encouragement to learn is an internal process. Students feel encouraged to learn when they feel responsible for learning and when they feel that they have some control over their learning. These two things go hand in hand. Students can learn to accept responsibility for their learning.

Responsibility for Learning. It's the student's responsibility to learn. A teacher who accepts sole responsibility for making students learn accepts an impossible task. Teachers are more likely to be effective when they share responsibility with students for their learning.

With little help or supervision from others, even small children can take responsibility for their own learning. In some nursery schools, children learn to wash clothes, stack blocks, experiment with paints, fix snacks, and more. Children are quite capable of taking responsibility for not being bored — provided that they are not over-managed. In an appropriate environment, children invent many excellent learning materials. Self-initiated activity is the biological norm. The similarity among babies, puppies, and kittens at play is quite striking. Boredom is not a problem; when bored, the infant mammal goes to sleep.

For most children, however, this has changed by the time the child enters kindergarten. While visiting a kindergarten in which the children were responsible for their own learning, choosing to work at whatever activity center interested them that day, I remarked about the atmosphere of cooperation, politeness, and intense activity. The teacher replied that this had changed from the beginning of the year. At first, many children had been afraid to do anything without the teacher's (mother's?) permission and had also been afraid of getting dirty, or playing with others, and so on.

In this particular kindergarten, although each child worked independently, the children functioned as a group. Materials were shared, and there was no fighting over equipment (such as easels) already in use. When one child spilled some paint, another helped to clean it up (the teacher was not around at the time). During group activities, the teacher usually had everyone's cooperation. The group represented a wide range of physical and social development, a wide range of interests and skills. Inevitable clashes (situations most teachers would call "discipline problems") were handled locally by the children themselves or by the teacher, without involving the whole class. Because of the diversity of activity, there was little chance that one student or a small group of students could disrupt the whole class. Like all students, the children tested the teacher and the situation in order to discover limits, as one graduate student found when he went to observe and ended up doing much of the work for a group of students. They knew better than to try to con the teacher, but found that they were able to con the grad student.

Some teachers may use the idea of a student's responsibility to avoid their own responsibility: "Well, if they want to learn, they'll learn." "If you're not interested, that's your problem." A teacher who makes this kind of remark is responsible for his or her own attitudes and behavior. Is this attitude likely to encourage students to learn? Wouldn't the teacher be more effective if he or she changed his or her attitudes?

Some teachers try to be entertainers. This seldom works very well because it places all the responsibility on the teacher and none on the students. Every teacher has experienced the discouragement of presenting something that seems interesting, only to have the presentation fall flat. The search for interesting material is a futile task; there is nothing that automatically interests everyone. Nothing in the world is interesting in itself. Someone must *take* an interest.

Boredom is learned. A small child is never bored. The most trivial object—a squashed paper cup, an empty beer can lying in the street, a cigarette butt—is often the object of intense interest to a small child. People who are bored often don't realize that things are not boring; rather, people feel bored.

A ten-year-old boy I worked with insisted that everything was boring. Nothing suited him and he felt very cheated that the world was not to his liking. He felt that he was powerless in a hostile environment, not realizing that *he* was responsible for much of his boredom and resentment.

"What Can You Do About It?" When students say that they're bored, instead of feeling defensive and trying to solve their problem, try Glasser's (1965) approach. Ask them, "What can you do about that?" or "What would you like to do about it?"

"What if," a teacher says, "it's really my fault that the students *are* bored?" It doesn't matter whose fault it is. Sharing the responsibility with students for making the class interesting is likely to have positive results.

You can't compete with television or other forms of entertainment, but you can do something much more powerful that TV

can't do: *You can structure the environment.* Don't try to enter-
tain; restructure your class so that you involve your students. An
interesting class is generally one in which everyone — teacher and
students — shares responsibility for what happens. We are most interested when we are involved, not when we are being entertained.

You can see it in classrooms, at workshops, in group encounter
sessions, in kindergartens, and in graduate classes: People of all
ages respond positively when they are actively involved in the
learning process — when they participate, do things, make things,
and share their ideas and opinions.

Encourage Students to Organize Their Own Activities. You
undoubtedly spend much of your day doing what other people
expect you to do as part of your job. They don't continually tell
you, however, exactly how to do everything and when to do it.
Some students feel that teachers are always on their backs, telling
them what to do. But you can try the following approaches to
increase students' control over their own learning:

1. Give students time to carry through on a project or request
   without your standing over them. Even if you're convinced
   that they'll do it wrong, back off. You can deal more
   effectively with a problem if you wait until the problem
   actually occurs. This may seem to contradict the oft-
   repeated phrase about stopping trouble before it starts. In
   reality, however, it is easy to create a problem by trying to
   avoid one.

2. Encourage students to organize their own activities where
   possible. Children whose time and activities are organized
   and managed by adults get little experience initiating and
   organizing even their free time. A simple example of this
   is a teacher who reported that he was asked by students to
   organize a basketball game for a group of students when
   he opened the gym on Sundays. It is difficult for many
   teachers to resist this type of request because it makes them

feel needed and useful. The students were quite capable of organizing their own pick-up game, so why shouldn't they be encouraged to do so?

Avoid Blame. At an early age, we learn that being trapped into admitting responsibility gets us into trouble. We quickly learn to protect ourselves by not admitting responsibility for what we say, think, feel, and do. Once we learn to avoid responsibility, we feel unwilling to accept responsibility for our own behavior.

People tend to refuse to accept responsibility when they equate accepting responsibility with accepting blame and with feeling guilty. A student denies responsibility for misbehaving, for doing poor work, or for not learning; a teacher denies responsibility for being unprepared, for not having test papers corrected, or for not teaching a difficult student; an administrator refuses to make clear-cut decisions, a parent. . .; and so on. All of us want to avoid blame and guilt. The emphasis on blame and guilt does not lead to improved behavior as often as it leads to the denial of responsibility. You can encourage students to accept responsibility if you avoid blaming them.

Model Acceptance of Responsibility. Teachers cannot expect students to accept responsibility for their actions when they are told, "You have to do this because it's a rule," or, "Because it's good for you." Rules, obligations, and policies don't just happen; someone decides what the rules are going to be, who has what obligations, and what the policies will be. It is dishonest to avoid responsibility for decisions by saying, "It's a school rule," or, "It's school policy." There is no "school" who makes decisions and policies; there are only people who make decisions and policies. If adults want kids to accept responsibility for their decisions, they must be willing to accept responsibility for their own decisions.

A child is told to eat spinach "because it's good for you." An adolescent is told to stay away from drugs "because it's against the law." The draftee is told to go to war "because we are forced to fight for freedom." In each case, a manmade order is made to appear natural and inevitable, as if people did not have a choice.

Of course that's the idea: By making decisions look as if they're not really decisions, it's easy to get people to go along with them. There are several problems with this approach: First, it's dishonest, thus encouraging and sanctioning dishonesty; and second, it's not effective because it models avoidance of responsibility.

Expect Students to Discount Your Good Intentions. Students quickly learn to distrust good intentions expressed by teachers, often because of bitter experience. The less you talk about creativity, open discussion, trust, and responsibility and use other words that have unfortunately become catch phrases, the more you can focus on doing activities that actually encourage these things. I don't expect students or clients to trust me until I've been found reliable and worthy of that trust in their eyes. The more difficult "problem" students often find it more difficult to trust teachers (as well as other students) and are likely to distrust even your best efforts.

Accept the Equality of Others as Responsible Persons. Equality is an ambiguous, easily misunderstood term. As applied here, however, its meaning is quite specific: No matter how knowledgeable, skillful, intelligent, right, insightful, or good I may be as a teacher, others have a right to make decisions and to be responsible for their behavior.

- Equality means accepting that, as a human being, I am no better or no worse than others, whether they are adults or children.

- Recognizing the equality of students frees the teacher from worrying about problems and responsibilities that belong to the students.

- Teachers who accept the equality of students are less likely to provide undue help.

- Teacher and student are equal in the sense that each is responsible for his or her behavior. We do not assume that a teacher's and a student's responsibilities are the same. Teachers are responsible for teaching. Students are responsible for learning, and they need to realize that they are responsible for learning if they're going to be successful learners.

SUMMARY

Teachers, like parents, have been taught to assume responsibility in areas that properly belong to the student. As a result, teachers easily find themselves embroiled in power struggles when they try to make students do what they're supposed to do. When teachers accept responsibility for problems that belong to the student, they discourage students from accepting responsibility.

Responsibility for learning belongs to the student, regardless of age. Kindergarten and graduate students alike can learn to take responsibility for their own learning. Teachers, however, usually unintentionally, tend to take the responsibility for imparting learning. (Indeed, they are often expected to do so.) When teachers assume responsibility that is not theirs, they invite manipulation by students. Fundamentally, encouraging students to learn means involving students in their own learning.

9
chapter

Coping With Power Struggles*

One student can't "remember" books and pencils. Another constantly bothers the teacher. Some children refuse to do assignments; others provoke fights. Teachers face such situations daily; how they handle these situations determines whether they find themselves in a power struggle.

For the past seven years, I have been teaching in-service teachers how to cope with power struggles. At the end of one workshop I led, a teacher expressed a typical attitude when she said, "I came

*Parts of this chapter originally appeared as "Focus on Self: An Approach to Using Dreikursian Principles to Cope with Power Struggles in the Classroom," *The Individual Psychologist*, 1979, *16* (2), 25-30.

here expecting to learn better ways to control children; what I learned instead is that I have to change myself." This teacher was restating a point that Dr. Rudolf Dreikurs, the famous Adlerian child psychiatrist, made in his classes. The only person you can change is yourself, but when you change yourself, others change in response. Teachers I have worked with generally find that the more they change themselves, the more effective they are in coping with power struggles.

CHANGING INTERPRETATION

For many teachers and parents, the first step in coping more effectively in the power struggle is to change the way they look at problem situations. Teachers typically see the issue in a power struggle as solving the problem at hand (e.g., getting students to complete assignments, maintaining discipline, or motivating students to learn). The real issue is often not the problem at hand (much as it may need a solution) but the struggle by both teacher and students to maintain their self-images, especially in regard to their power and status (Dreikurs, 1953, 1968).

Teachers and students often have conflicting ideas about their roles, and when this happens, a power struggle easily results. For example, it is important to some students to feel that they choose to act as they do. When teachers insist that these students obey simply because they are told to do so, the students feel threatened.

It is important for teachers to realize that their desire to be accepted and respected as authority figures is often in conflict with students' desires to question, to be independent, and to make their own decisions. A threat to either child or adult often results in feelings of fear and anger on both sides.

For example, when a student challenges a teacher's authority ("You can't make me be quiet!"), the teacher may easily feel threatened (internal response: "I'm losing control!") or angry (external response: "Sit down and shut up!"). Depending on how scared and how angry the teacher is, the student also feels scared and angry. These feelings are related to what the teacher and the student tell themselves about their roles in the group.

Become Aware of Your Internal Logic. For many teachers, maintaining position and status within the class means living up to a perfectionistic image of a good teacher. This is not as much an individual flaw as a socially maintained set of expectations that have become internalized. Teachers are encouraged to hold self-defeating, ineffective beliefs about themselves and their performance. An internal logic based on perfectionistic expectations might run like this:

> Major premise: Good teachers have good discipline and well-behaved students.
>
> Minor premise: I want to be a good teacher.
>
> Conclusion: When students don't behave, I'm not a good teacher (and I get upset, angry, frustrated, and can't stand it).

As Ellis (1975) points out, this kind of logic is irrational and leads to self-defeating behavior.

Students also have assumptions about maintaining their place in the group. For some students, maintaining their position means staying on good terms with authorities and avoiding behavior that adults find threatening. Other students may see their position in terms of avoiding control ("You can't make me!") or in terms of doing what they want ("I can do what I want"). These students may become rebellious or stubborn when confronted or when they don't get their own way. Yet both groups—those who conform and those who don't—have the same underlying goal: to achieve and maintain a place in the group.

Once the teacher realizes that all in the class—teacher and students alike—are in the same boat, the teacher can begin to step back and view the situation as a problem rather than as a threat.

Win or Lose Situations. For both teacher and students, finding themselves in a win-or-lose situation activates their internal logic and the feelings of fear and anger that accompany a threat. Power struggles arise out of situations where both teacher and students feel that, if they don't get their own way, they are losers and must feel bad about themselves. Losing is a threat to self-image, so neither side wants to give in, even where nothing is to be gained by fighting and winning.

The fact that there is a winner and a loser at the end of an episode in a power struggle creates an unstable situation that invites continuation of the struggle. One side may get its way in the short run, but in the long run, both sides suffer because the struggle over position and status in the group is never resolved. Once teachers see how a win-or-lose situation creates a struggle, they are in a position to change.

Win-or-lose situations are created by attitudes. A teacher writes as follows:

> Many teachers have been taught or have subscribed to what I call the "get them before they get you" theory. I've heard it and maybe said it myself before, "By God, no twelve-year-old is going to run over me." We feel that somehow the teacher must come out ahead in the end or look like a fool.

This attitude is irrational because there is no necessary connection between not winning and looking like a fool. The win-or-lose attitude is ineffective because it limits the teacher's options.

EFFECTIVE TEACHER BEHAVIOR

Reflect. Many teachers spend their energy trying to control students instead of focusing on what *they* could do to improve the situation. Since many situations occur over and over, teachers have many opportunities to ask themselves, "What could I do differently?" If nothing comes to mind, look at the interaction, asking, "What happened? What is the student getting out of the power struggle? Where have I been successful with this student, and how can I build on that? What has worked in similar situations?" Other teachers may help a teacher to find answers to these questions.

Listen. Teachers are often advised to listen, but they are seldom taught how. Many of the teachers find that Carl Rogers' listening technique of reflecting content and feeling has been extremely useful. Reflective listening helps teachers (1) to avoid moralizing, preaching, threatening, questioning, and other barriers to communication (Gordon, 1974) and (2) to become more perceptive listeners. Reflective listening also gives the students the feeling that they are understood, and this often leads to a new understanding of a problem situation by both sides.

Determine Responsibility. Many power struggles begin because a teacher feels responsible for student problems and behavior. Teachers are not responsible for solving every problem or correcting every misbehavior brought to their attention. When teachers assume responsibility for a student's problem, the student has little incentive to solve his or her own problems.

Withdraw Cooperation. Once teachers realize that power struggles are a form of negative cooperation, they are in a position to ask themselves, "What am I doing to cooperate in perpetuating this power struggle?" Once a teacher knows the answer to this question, the power struggle can often be ended by withdrawing cooperation. For example, teachers have asked me what to do about students who constantly ask questions. It had not occurred to them to simply ignore the questions because they did not see their replies as a form of cooperation.

Avoid Demands for Agreement. Some teachers hamper themselves by wanting students to agree that the teacher's actions are right, just, or fair. A teacher friend of mine said that she wanted students to say, "I want to do it," because this relieved her of guilt feelings. Teachers need to assume responsibility for making decisions, whether or not others agree. By insisting that others should agree, teachers invite a power struggle. Teachers can accept the opinions of others without being defensive by accepting their own responsibility to take action even though others disagree. This does not mean ignoring others' opinions or making decisions without taking others into account (which doesn't solve conflict) but rather being aware that others will not always agree that the teacher is right.

Encourage Students to Evaluate Their Behavior. It is important to help students become aware of their power to make situations better or worse. Students already exercise power, but often without being aware that they are making a choice or that they are responsible for that choice. Just as teachers can focus on their own behavior, they can encourage students to focus on *their* own behavior.

A head teacher in one of my classes reported that a class of junior high-school students he talked to blamed an assistant teacher for their misbehavior: "He doesn't make us behave." Whatever the assistant teacher's lack of skill in classroom management, the students did not realize that they also had responsibility for making the situation better or worse; therefore, they felt free to behave irresponsibly.

Here is a list of questions that can be used to encourage students to focus on their own behavior:

- "Are you making the situation better or worse?"
- "Are you helping the situation?"
- "Are you making the teacher a better or a worse teacher?"
- "What could you do to make the situation better? Worse?"
- "What could you do about it?"

It is important that these questions be asked without using a tone of voice that implies blame.

TEACHER ATTITUDES

Changes in behavior often produce changes in attitude; changes in attitude often produce changes in behavior. In practice, both evolve together. The focus in this section is on attitudes and their underlying logic.

Reduce Feelings of Defensiveness. Many teachers feel threatened or angry when their authority is questioned. I have heard teachers say about their students, "But they *should respect* authority." Perhaps teachers should get respect, but when they don't, feeling threatened makes a teacher less effective in dealing with a difficult situation. Teachers can be more effective when they see that their concern with how students *should* act is often a way of avoiding the immediate situation.

In a sense, feeling threatened is a form of cooperation. A student does something (intentionally or unintentionally) to threaten a teacher, and the teacher cooperates by feeling threatened. Teachers can learn to reduce their own feelings of defensiveness by changing their expectations from "I *have to* be treated a certain way, and students *have to* act in a certain way" to "I prefer that students behave in a certain way, but I'll cope with whatever behavior comes up."

Accept Others as Equals. Accepting others as equals means that we accept the right of others to act and to be responsible for their actions (including experiencing the consequences of those actions), however we may disagree with their actions. This means not shaming, blaming, lecturing, threatening, or inducing guilt, since these behaviors only serve to establish moral superiority without really focusing on the problem at hand.

Accepting students as equals is difficult because it means giving up the superior status that many teachers struggle to hold onto. Equality of status has tremendous payoffs, however, that more than make up for giving up a superior position. Equality frees teachers to deal directly with problem behavior instead of focusing on blame and guilt. Equality also frees teachers from accepting too much responsibility for a student's problem, thereby freeing the students to accept responsibility and to deal with the consequences of their actions.

Give Up the Myth of Control. Teachers are encouraged to believe that a good teacher can discipline, motivate, and otherwise control all students. This is a myth that makes many teachers less effective than they might be. In an effort to live up to the myth, they easily become drawn into power struggles or even actively provoke them without being aware of what they are doing. For example, consider a teacher who has the attitude, "No kid is going to get the best of me!" A student who insists on having the last word easily provokes such a teacher into a power struggle.

Some teachers may feel that they will have little credibility if the student does get the last word, but just the opposite is likely to be the case. Students, like other human beings, will tend to continue a behavior only if it gets results. The student who insists on having the last word achieves his or her goal only if having the last word means defeating the teacher. If the teacher does not feel or act defeated, the student has neither won nor lost the power struggle. Even when teachers know better, however, they often find that acting on their knowledge is difficult because they have difficulty giving up the myth that they *should* be able to demonstrate their control by having the last word.

From the time we enter kindergarten, we are taught to think that the teacher is supposed to be in control. No wonder that many teachers, after a lifetime of brainwashing, feel that they *have to* control everything that goes on and that they're failures if they don't. What we don't realize is that this way of thinking is like handing the students an invitation to defeat us by refusing to be controlled. Consider for a moment:

1. Doctors can't cure every patient.
2. Lawyers aren't expected to win every case.
3. Highway patrolmen can't stop accidents.
4. Psychiatrists can't make all their patients well.

These people are all dealing with probabilities. No matter how successful they are, they can't control the outcome of even a single case. They are effective not because they are in control but because they do what is most likely to result in success. Similarly, teachers cannot control their students. Even the most effective teacher has students who absolutely refuse to cooperate.

What is unfortunate about the myth that, as teachers, we should be able to control students, is that this myth leads us to be less effective, less successful, and less of an influence than we otherwise might be. Telling ourselves (or allowing others to tell us) that we *should be able to* or that we *have to succeed* in a particular endeavor almost always results in self-defeating behavior (Ellis, 1957, 1975, 1977, 1978).

The questions that seem to come up most when teachers discuss discipline are these:

1. How can I make the students do what they're supposed to do?
2. How can I make them behave?
3. How can I make them want to learn?

These questions all amount to the same thing; they ask basically the same question: "How can I be in control?" The answer is very simple, though not popular: You can't be in control; you can't make them do what they're supposed to do. However, the more skill you have in listening and problem solving, the more rapport you have and the more likely you are to be effective in winning the cooperation of the students.

COPING WITH
PROBLEM SITUATIONS

The following situations illustrate the principles discussed earlier.

A Case of Fighting. In this example, a sixth-grade teacher describes an incident where he found two boys fighting:

> Bang! Just as I walk in the door Monday morning, I find one boy in tears and one looking ready to explain the situation. Calmly, I asked both of them to come to my desk. Then I asked both of them what happened. Jon admitted punching Bill in the stomach (not *that* hard, he said) because Bill was shoving his desk. Bill said he shoved the desk because he was called a name. Then Jon said Bill had called him a name. All the while I listened intently, hoping to get the story straight.

Both boys calmed down after telling their stories. By listening without blaming or taking sides, the teacher was able to defuse the situation. It is extremely difficult, if not impossible, to get anyone—children or adults—to think and act rationally when they are upset. Also, unless the students feel understood, they are not likely to respond to the teacher's efforts to encourage them to evaluate their own behavior and decide what they could do about it:

> I asked each if the name-calling had helped them or each other. "No," was their answer. As for a plan [the teacher had asked what plan they could think of that would solve the problem in the future], they weren't sure. They both wanted their desks moved so they weren't so close, and they both wanted to apologize. I had them wait till the end of the day to discuss the moving of the desks —maybe they would change their minds. They both agreed that they could get along better with their desks moved, so I moved them.

The solution the boys came up with was acceptable to the teacher, but if it hadn't been, he could have asked for another plan, explaining that their solution was not acceptable. The teacher successfully avoided accepting responsibility for the problem, thus allowing the students to accept ownership of the problem. The teacher was encouraging responsibility far more effectively than he could have by using punishment. The question of punishment did come up later:

> Just before school was out, Jon talked to me. He was in a very serious mood. He thought that his punishment should have been more severe at the time. I guess that he is used to doing more than just talking things out and settling on his own plan. So we discussed harsh punishment and how it would help him. He decided that it really wouldn't have helped his behavior. I think students get used to a certain type of punishment. They expect it, and they don't expect to have a chance to tell their story and have someone listen.

Generally, the more punishment is used, the less effective it is. Punishment may make a strong impression at the time, but then it's over until the next time. Accepting responsibility and deciding what can be done to make a situation better, unlike punishment, implies a continuing commitment.

A final comment. Moving the desks may have brought the problem to a successful conclusion, but merely moving the desks would probably not have solved the problem. If the teacher had told the students to move their desks, we can imagine that they would have thought that they had gotten off easily and that they would have felt no responsibility for making the plan work.

A Case of Teacher Attitude Change. One of the myths of teaching is that teachers have no prejudices. In this example, the key to a more effective approach is a new awareness on the teacher's part of how a prejudice may lead to an unnecessary power struggle:

I had several run-ins with Tony, but since I've taken this class [a class for in-service teachers taught by the author] , things have really been improving. However, I hadn't really gained full trust in Tony. I'm sure this is part of the problem.

It was the first day of the fourth quarter, and we were changing seats. The desks are awkward to move, since they are large. The desks cause a commotion if they are slid across the floor, so the stuent must lift the desk enough to scoot it quietly across the floor. All students were able to do this satisfactorily, all but one — *Tony!* He was shoving his desk along, making a terrible racket, so I politely asked him to pick it up in order to get it to his new place. So he lifted it up, and all of his belongings slid out of the back, since the desks are open-backed. Five or six students laughed, and so did he. I told him to get to his new place and pick up his belongings in a hurry and to come up at noon to see me.

Noon rolled around, and he didn't show up , so I sent for him. When asked why he didn't show, he said that he didn't think he needed to because he had done nothing wrong. Whammo! I would have liked to pitch him right out into the yard, and I almost did. I could see that this was getting nowhere. I asked him to see me during study time.

At this point the teacher — the same teacher, by the way, who had handled the power struggle in the previous example so well — felt frustrated and could have easily precipitated a power struggle between himself and Tony. In an attempt to get Tony to shape up, the teacher could easily have ended up fighting with him. He would have won the verbal battle, but Tony would have been no closer to cooperating. Something else happened in the meantime:

Before study time, I ran into my wife, who is also a teacher, and she asked me about my day. I related the incident with Tony. She said that she thought I just didn't like Tony. His actions are truly at the bottom of my list, and my trust in him was next to zero.

The teacher decided to try listening when Tony returned:

We decided to talk in private in an empty office. I asked him to talk about the desk incident. He told me that it was truly an accident and that he felt that he had done nothing wrong. Then he began to cry [this was a sixth grader]. He said that I think everything he does is on purpose and that I wouldn't give him a chance! I let him talk for five to ten minutes. Soon he was thinking of ways he could improve his behavior in the classroom. I pledged equal cooperation, and we talked for thirty minutes.

The afternoon went fine. However, I'm proceeding with caution. I know that Tony needs support from the teacher. I hope that the crying and promises weren't just a ploy to get off the hook. I sure hope that if I'm giving him a fair chance to solve his problems, he will take this chance seriously.

At times, listening may seem almost like a magical solution, but the difficulty is that existing attitudes and feelings easily interfere with listening. What seems to be so easy in this example requires the teacher to become aware of and deal with his own prejudices.

Responding without Shock. Teachers are sometimes drawn into power struggles when students deliberately provoke a response. When the teacher acts upset or shocked, the student has succeeded. By not acting in the expected way, the teacher is much more likely to be effective. In the following example, a teacher describes a situation where he avoided a power struggle — actually, a series of power struggles — by *not* rising to a challenge to his authority:

I have had students try to use shock to pull me into power struggles. One girl, I remember, would try to appear very worldly and wise. She liked to bring in pornographic books and read them in class. She would hide them inside the cover of her textbook and then cause disruption in class by getting her neighbors to look at them. She was not very subtle about her actions, and I soon caught on to her game. Instead of acting shocked, I would simply pick up the book and place it in a desk drawer. Over the first quarter, I collected about ten books. When she finally stopped the practice, I was curious why. One day, I overheard her tell her lab partner that she sure was surprised

that I didn't get in an uproar when I found the books. It just wasn't
any fun when nothing happened.

The teacher was effective in this case for a number of reasons, perhaps the major one being that bringing the books in wasn't any
fun when the teacher didn't create an uproar. The teacher avoided
falling into the role of keeper of public morals by responding to
the problem as a distraction. Another reason the teacher was
successful was that he said little or nothing. Teachers often talk
too much, and the more they talk, the more they focus attention
on the situation.

Provide Choices and Consequences. In some problem situations, an
immediate consequence that students know about in advance can
be as effective as or more effective than discussion. In the following
example, an immediate consequence solved a problem that could
easily have become a power struggle. The example is based on a
story told by my wife, a junior-high science teacher at the time:

> On a spring day, many of the students brought water pistols to class.
> There was no way of knowing who was using them unless they were
> caught squirting their guns. The teacher told the first student she
> saw with a squirt gun that he had the choice of crunching the gun
> himself or giving it to the teacher to crunch. The student chose to
> crunch his own gun, as did most of the students caught with squirt
> guns. About six or eight guns were crunched during the first two
> days, and after that, no more guns were seen. Several times, students
> attempted to draw the teacher into a power struggle by saying, "So-
> and-so has one too," but the teacher replied, "I didn't see his [or
> hers]."

The students knew that squirt guns were considered contraband in
the school; also, the consequences of having the squirt guns visible
in class became known. By acting without moralizing or preaching,
the teacher avoided a power struggle. Another thing that helped to
avoid a power struggle was giving the students a chance to save

face by crunching their own guns. It was a chance, as the teacher put it, "to have one last bit of fun out of the guns." Some students made a big show of crunching them between their palms; others stepped on them. If the teacher had insisted that the students step on their guns, they would have seen this as punishment, but by giving them a choice, they were given a way of saving face. The teacher established a consequence for unacceptable behavior but also gave the students a choice about how the consequence was to be carried out.

SELF-DEFEATING
TEACHER ATTITUDES

Coping effectively with power struggles or avoiding them when they can be avoided is often difficult because of preconceived ideas about how teachers should act. When we aren't sure how to act, we easily slip into the role of teacher as moralist, judge, and authority figure or into the role of teacher as an unappreciated, resentful, frustrated, and angry individual who is unfairly expected to be all things to all people.

To a large extent, we generate and control our attitudes and our feelings by what we tell ourselves. By recognizing and then changing what we tell ourselves, we can more easily act effectively (Ellis, 1975, 1977).

In an unpublished paper written for one of my graduate classes, Gary Bell (1978) collected the responses of four teachers, two male and two female, to a situation involving a potential power struggle. Bell's study focuses on the feelings the teachers thought they would have when confronted with the following situation:

Larry, a student in your class, has requested to go to the restroom. You grant permission, and he leaves the room. At the end of five minutes, Larry has not returned. You step out into the hall and observe Larry in the parking lot with his car door open. When you question Larry about why he is at his car, he replies, "What's it to you?"

Teacher A. Teacher A has taught for twenty-five years, twelve years in a large urban school and thirteen in a small rural school.

QUESTION #1: How do you feel when you see Larry at his car?

TEACHER: My first reaction is anger. That idiot knows better than to do that with me. I'll make him regret doing it, and he will think twice before trying it again.

QUESTION #2: How do you feel when Larry says, "What's it to you?"

TEACHER: I feel like smacking him. No one talks back to me.

QUESTION #3: How do you describe your attitude as you confront Larry?

TEACHER: I am upset. This makes me feel like he has no respect for my authority. If I don't do something to impress upon him that he shouldn't do that with me, there is no telling what he will try next.

QUESTION #4: How has previous experience with similar situations influenced your feelings here?

TEACHER: These kids are always trying to pull something. I don't feel that I can trust them out of my sight. Some kid is going to try something just to get my goat.

QUESTION #5: How do those in authority influence your feelings?

TEACHER: I don't want to look like I'm not doing my job. I guess I do feel pressure.

This teacher is already in a power struggle when he sees Larry by his car. By defining himself as the authority figure who must be in control, he is setting himself up to be defeated. He seems to take Larry's actions as a personal affront. If he would confront Larry, Larry could defeat him by continuing to be smart or by just driving away. Or is the teacher going to try to restrain Larry physically and end up in a fight? In regard to those above him, the teacher feels that he must live up to an authority's idea of what his job is.

The teacher's attitude is not one that is likely to get much sympathy from readers. The teacher takes an aggressive attitude; he's out to get Larry; he's angry. Yet this teacher feels trapped by the expectations that he and others have of him. He feels responsible for making the students behave.

Teacher B. The second teacher is also male and has eight years' experience. His responses to Larry were as follows:

QUESTION #1: How do you feel when you see Larry at his car?

TEACHER: I feel like I have to do something, but I don't feel all that concerned.

QUESTION #2: How do you feel when Larry says, "What's it to you?"

TEACHER: I feel like I should really tell him off. This isn't any way for a student to talk to me.

QUESTION #3: How do you describe your attitude as you confront Larry?

TEACHER: I don't appreciate all the little dumb rules I have to keep constantly checking the kids on. It is a waste of time, and they should know how to behave enough to take care of themselves.

QUESTION #4: How has previous experience with similar situations influenced your feelings here?

TEACHER: It isn't the first time it has happened, and it probably won't be the last.

QUESTION #5: How do those in authority influence your feelings?

TEACHER: I am tired of having someone jump down my neck every time something goes wrong. Teachers are always blamed for not stopping something or for knowing that it was going on. What do they think I am, anyway?

The teachers were given only the one paragraph about Larry, which makes no mention of authority figures. Teacher B, like Teacher A, seems to accept responsibility for living up to an impossible standard. If an authority figure expects them to live up to this impossible standard, Teachers A and B make it their problem. Thus they end up feeling pressure from both sides: from the students because they're trying to force the students to behave, and from the administrators because they're trying to live up to an impossible standard. They are bound both to feel frustrated and to end up in power struggles because they're trying to be in control.

Teachers need to realize that when administrators do pressure them to accept responsibility for controlling students rather than holding students accountable for their own behavior, they can remain the judge of their own behavior. They still have a problem with the administrator, but their problem is how to deal with an uptight administrator rather than how to live up to the administrator's expectations. Once the teacher realizes that if the administrator is upset, that's the administrator's problem, he or she can deal with the administrator in a rational way, using listening and assertive skills effectively. Straightening out in one's own mind the relationship between teacher and authority can be extremely useful in coping more effectively with students. When teachers realize that they are responsible not for controlling student behavior but for responding in a rational and professional manner, they can begin to focus on their own behavior and how they can change it.

Teacher B indicates that he would feel like telling Larry off. This is a typical reaction that we have all had at one time or another. Unfortunately, this attitude, no matter how natural or correct it might seem, opens the teacher up for a royal battle. Instead of responding in a mature way, the teacher is likely to tell Larry off in a way that invites additional comments from Larry. The teacher is more likely to be effective if he doesn't respond to Larry's invitation to get into a power struggle.

Teacher C. Teacher C is female, has three years' teaching experience, and is twenty-five. She responded as follows:

QUESTION #1: How do you feel when you see Larry at his car?

TEACHER: I first feel angry. This changes to disappointment that he lied to me. I feel like I have been used.

QUESTION #2: How do you feel when Larry says, "What's it to you?"

TEACHER: I feel hurt that he would do this. I am disappointed and shocked when a student behaves toward me in a hostile manner.

QUESTION #3: How do you describe your attitude as you confront Larry?

TEACHER: I don't really know. I am not uptight, but I am anxious to avoid a harsh scene. I really dread these confrontations.

QUESTION #4: How has previous experience with similar situations influenced your feelings here?

TEACHER: Yes, it does affect me. I remember how things have gone before when I have confronted a student. It makes me try to keep my control.

QUESTION #5: How do those in authority influence your feelings?

TEACHER: I feel like the principal pressures us to get control. This causes me to be more harsh than I really think the situation merits.

There are two things that stand out in these answers. First, the teacher is concerned with feeling hurt and shocked. Feeling hurt or shocked is a way of taking a situation personally and is unlikely to lead to effective behavior. Students do ditch school; the teacher's decision to confront the student is a reasonable one, though she might have chosen not to. By taking the confrontation personally, she makes the situation a win-or-lose situation. By deciding to feel hurt, she decides that she has already partly lost. The second thing that stands out is the teacher's feeling that she is not responsible for making her own decisions. She feels that the principal is unduly affecting her decisions. If the principal is putting pressure on her, she does have a problem that she needs to deal with. Her answers indicate that, to some extent, she is allowing the principal to be the judge of her actions. Letting the principal do this is not likely to make her more effective with the students, nor will it increase the principal's respect for her. Finally, and perhaps most important, she is likely to lose confidence in her own judgment and ability to act effectively.

Teacher D. Teacher D is also female and has fourteen years' teaching experience. She answered this way:

QUESTION #1: How do you feel when you see Larry at his car?

TEACHER: Mad. I feel very upset because this could get me in trouble, too.

QUESTION #2: How do you feel when Larry says, "What's it to you?"

TEACHER: Shocked. I never expect a student to talk back to me. It sets me on my heels.

QUESTION #3: How do you describe your attitude as you confront Larry?

TEACHER: Less angry than I was and dreading doing it, because I will just be acting like a teacher.

QUESTION #4: How has previous experience with similar situations influenced your feelings here?

TEACHER: Past experience with this type of behavior has always been unpleasant to me. I try to avoid getting into these fixes.

QUESTION #5: How do those in authority influence your feelings?

TEACHER: Sure, it influences my feelings. I know what the board members would say if I couldn't handle it effectively.

The teacher's first statement is a strong "I" statement and could be very effective in confronting Larry without making it into a win-or-lose situation. In subsequent answers, the teacher talks about shock at Larry's language, her dread of confronting him, and her fear of what the school board will say if she isn't effective. There is a feeling that the teacher is more on the spot than Larry. Although all of these emotions are understandable, none of them will help the teacher act effectively.

Acting from a Position of Strength. Trying to please others, trying to control others, or trying to do both at the same time — please authorities and control students — puts the teacher in a position of weakness. The only true position of strength is to be the judge of one's own behavior and to focus on making that behavior as effective as possible. Confronting a situation in a direct way without being aggressive puts the teacher in a position of strength, because no matter what the student does, the teacher is unlikely to prolong the struggle.

In the situation with Larry, Larry may decide to leave, regardless of what the teacher does. Trying to control Larry's behavior only invites Larry to defeat the teacher by leaving. If the teacher feels that he or she needs to confront Larry, he or she might let Larry know how he or she feels and remind Larry what the consequences of his actions are likely to be, while making it clear to Larry that he is responsible for his own behavior.

In the first three examples discussed in this chapter, the teachers described how they handled situations so that the students didn't feel like they were in a win-or-lose situation. The discussion of Larry and the responses of the four teachers indicate that it is equally important that teachers avoid placing themselves in situations where they, the teachers, lose. The attitudes of all four teachers indicate that they might feel obligated to put themselves in positions where they would be losers because of the pressure from authority. It is essential that teachers accept responsibility for being the judge of their own behavior so that they can avoid power struggles.

SUMMARY

Teachers cannot force cooperation, nor can they totally eliminate power struggles. The myth that the teacher can or should control students makes many teachers less effective in coping with power struggles and often leads to feelings of fear and anger. Yet, by focusing on changing their interpretation of events, their behavior in response to those events, and their attitudes, teachers can cope effectively with power struggles.

10
chapter

Encouraging a Sense of Group Through Group Discussion

Much of the work of encouragement can take place in group discussion. Group discussion can help create a feeling of belonging, an atmosphere of cooperation and problem solving, and a willingness to listen and to share ideas and feelings. Group discussion plays a central role in the classroom management approaches of Dreikurs (1968), Dreikurs, Grunwald, & Pepper (1971), Glasser (1969), Gordon (1974), and Rogers (1969).

In his last book, Dreikurs summed up the human condition in these words: "Man is a social being. His basic desire is to belong. Only if one feels one belongs can one function, participate, contribute" (Dreikurs, 1971, p. ix). Belonging is a sense of having a place, having the feeling, "I belong." Dreikurs writes, "Alfred Adler described this basic human desire to belong as *Gemein-*

schaftsgefuehl, which can be roughly translated as social interest, a sense of communion, of feeling that one is embedded in the stream of life, of concern for the welfare of others" (Dreikurs, 1971, p. ix).

In reading these sentences, one gets the feeling that somehow the words don't quite express the meaning; there is no way to express in a few words the sense of relatedness to the world and other people. We know that those who don't have a sense of belonging will not cooperate and cannot easily be encouraged to do so. William Glasser expressed a similar idea in one of his lectures when he said that responsibility is the ability to give and receive love. By this he meant that people who have a sense of caring and being cared for act in a responsible and caring way toward those who care and are cared for by them. Adler and Dreikurs might have put it this way: Responsibility and cooperation flow from social interest, from concern for others, and from a feeling of belonging.

Students who rebel, who refuse to cooperate, or who withdraw are the students who are likely to feel that they don't belong, that no one likes them, and that they have little power to change what happens to them. Such students may be coerced into conforming, but without a change in their feeling of not belonging, they are unlikely to cooperate.

Too often, students don't feel that they belong because they are intentionally or unintentionally excluded from the group and are treated with condescension by teachers and other students. There are few schools where both teachers and students are not aware of certain individuals or groups who are rejected by teachers and students alike because of their behavior, their attitudes, their ancestry, their race, their social status, their run-ins with the police, their family reputation, and so on. In a tightly knit community, just being the new kid in town may be enough to exclude a child—especially if he or she is in any way different from the other students.

Methods of teaching and discipline that exclude the child from feeling that he or she belongs—especially those methods that enlist the support of the "good" students on the teacher's side—create or at least maintain existing problems.

Belonging Is Unconditional. True belonging is unconditional: We belong by reason of our existence; we belong to such-and-such a family by reason of our birth; we belong to such-and-such a society by reason of having been born into it; we belong to the universe by reason of being part of it (Dreikurs, 1971). Belonging is not something that can be earned; otherwise, it isn't belonging. A sense of belonging is essential in creating cooperation because when problems do come up, it provides a basis on which to solve those problems. A child who misbehaves but feels that he or she is still a part of the group, whether it's a family group, a school group, or a group of friends, is much more likely to take correction and cooperate than one who feels that he or she is no longer a part of the group. Encouraging a feeling of belonging can best be accomplished by integrating everyone into the group (Dreikurs, 1968).

In working as a co-facilitator in a teen therapy group one year, what I seemed to hear most often was that the group members felt that they didn't belong. Some were good students, and some were not; but they all felt that they had no one they could talk to outside the group. They felt that they didn't really belong. In particular, those who came from small communities felt that they had been labeled inferior or crazy (for using drugs or attempting suicide) by the whole community—including those in their own age group. Far from rejecting family and school, they seemed desperately to want to belong and be accepted.

The group members did, however, feel accepted in the group; they felt a sense of belonging in the group. It would be easy to assume that this feeling of belonging came from the fact that they all agreed with one another. They understood how someone could try to commit suicide (most had tried), take drugs, skip school, or stay out late (which most had also done), but they didn't support each other in these behaviors; in fact, they were often very confrontive with each other over one another's destructive feelings and actions. The co-therapists were also often confrontive.

The feeling of belonging in the group was, I believe, generated out of the feeling of acceptance. Acceptance and agreement are two different things. Group members didn't have to worry about being rejected. Others would listen, and even if they didn't agree, they would not pass judgment.

Why a Sense of Group Is Important. Developing a sense of group is an important goal:

- Establishing a sense of group does not eliminate problems, but it does provide a mechanism for solving problems. Solving problems often depends on creating cooperation *among* students as well as *between* teacher and students.

- Individual learning as well as a willingness to explore, to be creative, and to try new things requires the security of having a place and being accepted.

- A sense of group encourages cooperation that goes far beyond mere conformity to rules. Students may conform so as not to get into trouble, yet they may defeat the teacher by making mistakes unnecessarily, by opposing the teacher in little ways, or by being too good. Cooperation, on the other hand, is much more likely to result in both teachers and students meeting their needs.

- A sense of group allows a teacher to share responsibility. A teacher who tries to do everything—to solve all problems—tries to do the impossible and ends up feeling frustrated. A sense of group allows the responsibility for solving problems to rest with the group.

- A sense of group allows students to help one another and to solve many problems among themselves without needing to go to the teacher.

- A sense of group encourages the individual's sense of responsibility even when he or she is away from the group. Even when students are working on a project alone—for example, at home or in the library—the sense of responsibility to the group and the feeling of support received from the group influence their actions.

- A sense of group provides a feeling of support for teacher and students.

GENERAL PRINCIPLES OF
ENCOURAGING A SENSE OF GROUP

Using a Circle. Sitting in a circle encourages students to interact more freely (Dreikurs, 1968; Dreikurs, Grunwald, & Pepper, 1971; Glasser, 1969).

- A circle allows group members to see and be seen, to hear and be heard.
- In a circle, the teacher may still be a center of attention, but the teacher is in a much better position to allow others to be the center of attention when they speak. One measure of a successful group is the extent to which group members talk with one another and to the group rather than addressing themselves to the teacher.
- In a circle, everyone is exposed; no one can hide behind furniture or other people. At first, this may be threatening to some members who would prefer to hide or who don't want to reveal what they think or feel, but when those who feel threatened find that they are accepted and not put down, they will feel more secure and will be more willing to participate than when they are seated in rows.

Relinquishing Control. The nature of group discussion requires the group leader to avoid trying to control what happens. Attempts to steer discussion according to plan seldom work. A group leader must be willing to relinquish control and not try to act as a chairman. This can be very frustrating at times, especially if you do have something you would like to accomplish, but if you try to force discussion, everyone will clam up, and then you're stuck. On the other hand, when you begin to see that you really *can't* control what happens, you are in a much better position to relax and trust the group.

Encouraging Participation. When three or four people monopolize group time, the group can easily become an audience. What can be done about too much talking by some?

- Whenever possible, turn the problem back to the group: "It seems we have a problem — a lot of people aren't talking at all. How do you feel about that?"
- Ask students who do talk a lot to monitor how much group time they use.
- When students who don't usually talk look like they want to say something, don't be afraid to invite them to speak. "You look like you have some strong feelings about that, John." Or, "John?" may do just as well.
- Talk to students who are monopolizing group time individually and in private, asking them to help encourage others to speak by not speaking as much.

Listening as Participation. Being a member of a group implies participation. But what is participation? Being a good listener is as important as being a good talker. Those who seldom talk may be learning a great deal.

GROUP DISCUSSION

We may divide group discussion into three types:

1. *Problem-solving discussions* concerned with making decisions and solving problems.
2. *Sharing discussions* concerned with sharing ideas, feelings, values, and experiences.
3. *Subject matter discussions* concerned with subject-oriented tasks.

In practice, I find that these are to some extent interchangeable. A subject-oriented discussion may lead to a sharing of experiences. A sharing discussion may lead to a synthesis of subject matter material with personal experience. A problem-oriented discussion about when to hold an exam, how to do a paper, or how to deal with disruptive talking often involves sharing of feelings. And so on. I have divided group discussion into these three categories because a teacher's role is somewhat different for each.

Rules. A minimum number of rules may be needed to keep the class functioning as a group. These rules should be agreed upon by everyone, and group members should discuss and help to make the rules. The rules that are needed are little more than a formalization of common courtesy. Here are two examples of rules that work well:

1. *One person speaks at a time.* Reasons are obvious.
2. *If someone wants to disagree, he or she states his or her opinion without accusing, blaming, or insulting the other person, preferably using "I" sentences.* Group members feel more willing to talk when they know that those who disagree will say, "I see it this way...," or, "I think that..." instead of, "How can you say that?", or "You haven't thought about such-and-such," or, "Do you really believe that...?"

PROBLEM-SOLVING DISCUSSIONS

Problem-solving discussions are a way of sharing responsibility with the class. Such discussions might be about behavior problems (a big concern of teachers), about when and how students are to be evaluated (a big concern of students), about setting up workable rules (a big concern of both), and so on.

In order to win cooperation and arrive at workable solutions, discussions need to be democratic — that is, solutions are arrived at cooperatively rather than being imposed from on high.

Different authors suggest a different number of steps in problem solving, but they all include the following in one form or another, not necessarily in this order:

1. Statement of the problem.
2. Listening to what everyone has to say.
3. Suggestion of possible solutions.
4. Evaluation of solutions.
5. Agreement on a solution.

Let's consider these elements one at a time.

Statement of the Problem. When the teacher owns a problem, he or she can say, "I have a problem" and then explain what it is.

Another effective approach is to use Gordon's (1974) three-part "I" message (see earlier discussion in Chapter 7).

Here are two examples of teachers using an "I" message to state a problem:

- "When people are milling around after the bell rings, I feel frustrated because we don't get started on time, and then we have trouble finishing on time, too.
- "When the room is a mess at the end of class, I feel really upset because I don't like to clean up the mess."

It is important that these sentences be said in a tone of voice that communicates that the teacher feels strongly about the matter without, however, blaming, accusing, or trying to make students feel guilty. Students are expecting to be blamed and shamed as soon as the teacher even brings up the subject, so it is important that the teacher be especially careful about his or her tone of voice. If at all possible, do not bring the matter up for discussion when you're already upset, because then it is extremely difficult to carry on a rational discussion.

Not all problems are teacher-owned problems. By sharing the

responsibility for the planning and organization of learning with the students, teachers can draw the students more actively into the learning process. Unfortunately, this is one area where teachers find it difficult to share responsibility. By doing so, however, teachers can encourage motivation and commitment to learning. Some examples follow:

1. *Discussion of how work is to be evaluated.* Of course, the teacher has the right to decide how students are to be evaluated; on the other hand, I've found that students will willingly do things that they have chosen to do, whereas they actively resist those same things when I impose them. For example, many students resist writing papers, yet many teachers feel that students need to do more writing. By proposing that an evaluation could be an exam or something else, and then by asking the class for help in considering alternatives, even students who don't like to write may suggest or at least agree to write a paper, to do a presentation, or to work on a project in place of taking an exam.

2. *Discussion of how to organize a group project.* This doesn't have to be done as a whole class. Once students have learned through class discussion how a discussion is conducted, small groups are usually capable of handling their own discussions.

Listening to What Everyone Has to Say. Use the techniques of reflective listening, including paraphrasing and summarizing without evaluating or judging what's being said. People won't talk if they feel put on the defensive. Avoid questioning as much as possible. Don't agree or disagree. If you agree, people who have another view may be reluctant to share their thoughts. If you disagree, the person you're listening to, and other group members as well, may be reluctant to share their thoughts. You'll have plenty of time to state your ideas and position later on.

Reflective listening is particularly useful when students challenge the teacher or the teacher's authority. Using reflective listening defuses the challenge by incorporating it into the discussion without giving it undue emphasis by arguing. Here is an example:

STUDENT: This is dumb. You're supposed to be the teacher.

TEACHER: (Select one) You feel uncomfortable trying to solve this. You think this is a dumb way to decide things. You would prefer me to make the decision.

Any of these responses might be effective in defusing the situation, provided that they are said in a sincere, concerned tone of voice without threat, defensiveness, or sarcasm.

Suggestions of Possible Solutions. The solutions need to come from the students. If the teacher makes the suggestions and then tries to sell a solution, the students may agree to go along, but they won't feel much commitment and are less likely to follow through. Of course, the teacher may want to suggest a solution and has every right to do so, but if the teacher waits until the students have made their suggestions, they will have had a chance to offer their suggestions without undue pressure. By waiting, there is also a good chance that the teacher's ideas will already have been suggested by students.

Some teachers may want to write a list of all possible solutions on a blackboard, as suggested by Gordon (1974). Smaller classes can usually function quite well informally without recording solutions; larger classes may benefit from having suggestions written down so that everyone can see them.

Evaluation of Possible Solutions. Evaluation of solutions needs to come *after* everyone has had a chance to give an opinion. No matter how silly, impossible, or unrealistic a solution may seem, treating it the same as other ideas will prevent the group (and the teacher) from getting sidetracked. Evaluating solutions needs to be done carefully so that no one (especially the teacher) sabotages the discussion process. The following steps are useful, although these steps are seldom clear-cut; they tend to take place simultaneously:

1. *Eliminating unacceptable solutions.* Solutions that would be against school rules or are against the law are unacceptable (Gordon, 1974), and very few students will argue the fact; in fact, they can't argue unless the teacher argues with them. Usually, such solutions are proposed in order to see what the teacher is going to do.

   A solution needs to be acceptable to the teacher. If the teacher is not willing to go along with a solution, he or she can simply say, "I'm not willing to go along with such-and-such."

   A solution that is unacceptable to a class member or members needs to be rejected. This, in effect, gives individuals veto power over any solution. This can create real problems, but it is important in achieving group harmony. If some members of the class feel that they are being forced into a decision that they really can't accept, they are likely to undermine cooperation.

2. *Eliminating punishment.* Particularly when a group is working on a problem that involves misbehavior, students will suggest punishment. They are so used to punishment that they accept it as a fair way to handle many problems. When this happens, teachers can encourage students to reconsider punishment in a nondirective, nonblaming tone of voice: "Will this help the situation?" or "Will punishment help people cooperate?" or "Will punishment make the situation better for all of us?" Usually, at least a few students will begin to realize that punishment really doesn't work very well and that punishment doesn't really improve behavior most of the time.

3. *Making a list of possible, acceptable solutions.* Usually, one or more solutions will emerge as possible and acceptable.

Agreement on a Solution. Perhaps this is the most difficult step. It is often a mistake even to try to find a solution that everyone prefers, because individuals seldom agree on their preferences. It is important to realize that everyone needs to agree on a solution but that the solution need not be the solution that they would prefer. This is terribly important, because otherwise a discussion can end in frustration and stalemate, with nothing accomplished.

1. *Consensus.* If at all possible, the group works until consensus is achieved. Consensus is much more difficult to achieve than a majority, but it is important not to split the class into two groups—winners and losers. Even if the group of losers in a vote is very small, those students are likely to feel left out, imposed upon, or treated unfairly. For this reason, it is usually more effective to avoid voting on an issue. Straw polls, however, can be useful in helping solutions to emerge. In a small group, this usually isn't necessary, because everyone usually knows what everyone else thinks by the time they are ready to make a decision. In a group of twenty or more, however, straw polls can be very useful. Here is a sample of the types of questions I have found useful:

● How many people prefer "X"? How many prefer "Y"?
● Does anyone find "X" unacceptable? How about "Y"?

2. *Majority rule.* Having just given good reasons why it's important to work for consensus, I have to admit that I sometimes do rely on majority rule to make certain decisions. For example, I sometimes give students a choice of exam dates, especially when the exam falls near a vacation (Thanksgiving, Easter) or near a special event (home-

coming). If possible, once solutions have been narrowed down to two or three possibilities, all of which are acceptable to everyone—including the teacher, of course—I will take a vote, and majority rules.

Time Factors. Anyone who has ever been a member of a committee that tried to make a decision knows how difficult it is and how *long* it takes to make a decision. However, the process is itself a learning experience. People get to know one another, get to know the issues involved, and develop a sense of responsibility for the group and for the decisions they make. When teachers see this process as a learning experience rather than as something to get over as quickly as possible so that they can do some *real* teaching, they are more likely to be effective in group discussion.

Sometimes material on group problem solving may encourage teachers to make problem solving overly long and involved; when this happens, students become bored or frustrated. Many decisions can be made quickly. Here are some suggestions I have found helpful in avoiding overly long discussions.

1. If you already know before you start that there are only two solutions that are acceptable to you, state them, and then proceed through the steps.

2. Decisions regarding small-group projects can best be done in small groups. Students can divide up into small groups that can work simultaneously.

3. Structuring the problem before you start group discussion can be useful, especially where students need a place to start from. For example, wherever possible, I like to give people choices to think about. These choices may end up changed, modified, or even rejected, but presenting them at the beginning is often useful in getting problem solving off the ground.

4. Remembering that methods found in books (including this book) are suggestions, not rules, may help teachers to

avoid a long problem-solving discussion when a short one is enough. A sense of priorities is essential. Don't spend an hour on solving a problem that is not a high priority to either teacher or students. On the other hand, don't spend five minutes on a problem that teacher and students feel strongly about.

SHARING DISCUSSIONS

Sharing discussions are discussions that encourage the sharing of ideas, feelings, values, problems, and personal concerns. They are not intended to solve problems, and no evaluations are made. Sharing discussions emphasize listening.

Teacher's Role. The teacher's role is basically nondirective. In a problem-solving discussion, the teacher's role is to lead the group to find a solution. In a sharing group, the teacher's role is to listen and to encourage others to listen without evaluating or judging others. The appropriate communication skills are those that have already been thoroughly discussed:

- Reflective listening, including paraphrasing and summarizing.
- Avoidance of questions and evaluations.
- Encourage students to use "I" statements.

Participation. It is essential that everyone participate. If some students hang back and don't participate, others will stop participating because they feel like they're on stage in front of an audience. This is not so much a problem in the elementary school, but in junior and senior high, students are very conscious of the responses of other students and won't talk if they don't feel supported by the rest of the group.

Participation can't be forced. It can be encouraged, however. Here are some techniques that are useful in encouraging participation without forcing it:

1. *The right to pass.* Everyone has the right (whether or not it's always observed by others) to pass on answering questions regarding values, personal problems, or personal concerns. It is unethical to coerce anyone into talking about or sharing anything he or she doesn't want to. I have been in groups where everyone was expected to "produce," and I strongly resented it. Don't push.

   The right to pass can be used as a technique to encourage participation. I sometimes ask people before we start a group discussion to say, "I pass" if they don't want to answer a question. By saying "I pass," they are participating as group members, even when they don't have anything to share. This may sound trivial, but saying, "I pass" involves at least a minimal commitment to the group, and it tends to draw that person into the group.

2. *Values voting.* This technique (Simon, Howe, and Kirschenbaum 1978) is a good way to get participation from everyone without creating a threat. The leader asks everyone to take a nonverbal stand on a question involving values, personal preferences, interests, or opinions. In effect, the teacher is taking a poll. Students are asked to respond by raising their hands or putting their thumbs up (meaning, "I agree"), putting their thumbs down (meaning, "I disagree"), or folding their arms (meaning, "I pass"). This technique is useful in building trust in the group process. It does not require a large risk, and it involves everyone. This technique differs from ordinary hand-raising polls in that it draws in those who don't want to declare themselves by asking them to fold their arms. Once students begin to participate, few students will fold their arms for every question. The arm folding is a form of "I pass" and is a legitimate answer to any question involving values and feelings.

3. *Process whips.* In a process whip (Simon, Howe, and Kirschenbaum, 1978) group members respond very quickly to

a question or statement. One person starts, and then the other members of the group respond at random or by going around the circle. (Responding at random usually takes longer, but it also gives members a chance to think and respond on their own initiative.) "I pass" is a legitimate response.

SUBJECT MATTER DISCUSSIONS

In *subject matter discussion*, the teacher is in a more traditional role. In subject matter discussions, the teacher can provide expertise and guidance, lead discussions, and challenge students to think. The difficulty is leading without cutting off discussion. "Discussion classes" seldom turn out to have much discussion. The class is often monopolized by the teacher and three or four students. It's happened in my undergraduate class, out of desperation rather than ignorance. Getting a group — especially a large group of thirty or more — to talk can be extremely difficult. Elementary-school teachers are not often faced with groups of this size, but junior-high and high-school teachers are.

General Principles. The general principles for encouraging subject matter discussions are the same as those for all discussions: being a good listener while avoiding image-centered criticism, humiliation, or ridicule. The most common reasons I have heard students give for not participating are that they don't have anything to say, that they're afraid of looking foolish, or that they can't think of anything profound or impressive. In other words, they feel self-conscious; they feel as though they're on stage, as we all have at one time or another when asked to speak in front of a group of our peers. Yet these same students would have to admit that not having anything to say seldom stops them from talking with their friends. The difference is that people don't feel as though they're speaking to an audience when they're with friends. When people feel they're part of a group, they feel much less self-conscious about speaking because they feel belonging and acceptance.

Willingness to think, to challenge and be challenged, and to evaluate ideas is much more likely to take place where people feel acceptance and belonging. Teachers who listen and take students seriously without putting them down are able to communicate acceptance of the person without having to accept or agree with the individual's ideas, interpretations, or attitudes.

Waiting. The average time a teacher waits for a response is on the order of one second (Rowe, 1974). If students don't reply, many teachers repeat, rephrase, ask a different question, or call on another student (Rowe, 1974, p. 81). When teachers achieve a mean wait time of three to five seconds, the quantity and quality of responses increase (Rowe, 1974). (See also Chapter 4, *Student Strategies.*)

Asking Vague Questions. Vague questions, such as "What would you like to learn about?", can be a challenge that leads to growth and exploration; on the other hand, vague questions are more likely to produce uneasiness, suspicion, or frustration. When a teacher asks such questions without any preparation, students are likely to respond with blank stares. Similarly, invitations to "be as creative as you like" or to "do whatever you want" are likely to leave students with a sense of uneasiness and insecurity. Asking for opinions ("What do you think about 'X'?") or reactions "How did you react to the movie?") may stimulate discussions, but I haven't had much luck with them unless I was working with a group of highly motivated, interested students who wanted to talk even before being asked.

Open-Ended, Specific Invitations vs. Closed Questions. Closed questions that can be answered "yes" or "no" close off discussion rather than inviting it; such questions are too specific. On the other hand, questions that are general may be open-ended, but they don't give the group a structure to work with. Questions that are both specific *and* open-ended are often effective, providing structure without defining what can be said. Let's look at examples of different questions:

- Did you like the book? [Too specific; invites a yes or no answer].
- Tell us about the book. [Too general].
- What did you like about the book? [Open-ended and specific].
- What did you dislike? [Open-ended and specific].
- Name two things you will take away with you from reading the book. [Open-ended and specific].

The examples given of open-ended, specific questions are not profound questions; rather, they are invitations to speak about what concerns the individual student. When this approach is successful, students will often raise questions and problems that I would want to raise in a serious discussion.

Pencil and Paper. Asking students to write on a question, especially a specific, open-ended question, is a useful technique to use before beginning a discussion. It gives students a chance to collect their thoughts, and having a piece of paper in hand provides security — no one has to worry about not having anything to say. After students have had five minutes or so to write, ask them to share their ideas. Encourage them to speak without reading from their papers. Once they've organized their thoughts and have the paper as a security blanket, many students won't even need to look at their papers.

Sentence Completion. Providing a sentence stem to be completed by the student verbally is a good way to get a large number of responses in a short time. For example, see the following:

- "I liked . . ."
- "An idea I found use ful was . . ."
- "An idea I'll remember is . . ."
- "I disliked . . ."
- "I never knew that . . ."
- "I learned that . . ."
- "I would like to know more about . . ."

Once students have gotten through the first sentence, they often find it easy to expand on what they've said.

Small Groups. Dividing a class into small groups of two, three, four, five, or six people to complete a task that requires discussion is an effective way of increasing participation. Students who feel nervous about speaking in a large group will usually talk in small groups. Assigning shy students to the same group and the most willing participants to another group can be an effective way of encouraging participation by putting more assertive students together.

Switching Small Group Members. Using many short discussions where students continually switch groups so that, over a period of days or weeks, every student has worked with every other student in a small group is an effective way of encouraging openness and trust in the class as a whole.

Combining Techniques. Techniques can be effectively combined. Serious discussion can't be forced. On the other hand, providing structure by using these techniques will help students to feel secure while, at the same time, building a sense of group. When students don't like a group, using short, structured exercises; using pencil and paper; using sentence completions, and using small groups can be effective in giving teacher and students confidence in group discussion. Classes that develop a sense of group can conduct serious discussions for long periods of time with little structure. Such discussions, when they happen, make teaching stimulating and worthwhile. However, students must usually be taught to function as a group. Building a sense of group may take months of work. Don't expect group techniques to work overnight. Don't be discouraged when they don't always work. Trust and openness are usually built up over a long period of time, and they can't be rushed. When they are achieved, the results can be intellectually and emotionally satisfying.

Some critics of the schools claim that teachers spend too much time in preparing students to be well adjusted and too little time challenging them intellectually. If by this they mean that teachers spend too much time trying to get students to behave and conform, I would agree. On the other hand, teachers who encourage students to share ideas, feelings, concerns, and even personal problems and who encourage students to accept one another and to cooperate are creating an environment where students can take learning seriously and can put their energy into thinking and learning rather than into protecting themselves and feeling self-conscious.

Working with a group as a group leader is a skill. You learn how to be a group leader by doing it, by experimenting, by taking risks, and by making mistakes. Many teachers who try to allow more freedom in their classes close the door to greater responsibility and freedom for their students when they find that students do not know how to respond. Students must be trained how to respond to a new set of expectations. When a class finally establishes a sense of group, the change may seem instantaneous, but the process of reaching this goal is often a long and difficult struggle.

SUMMARY

Group discussion where students feel free to say what they think and how they feel is essential for creating a sense of group. Many teachers feel that group discussion is worthwhile, but they may also feel that they just don't have the time for it. The advantages of group discussion often more than make up for any time lost:

- Group discussion helps to create a sense of group. This can help to eliminate many problems before they come up.
- Group discussion provides a mechanism for solving problems.
- Group discussion provides a mechanism for exploring ideas, attitudes, and values.
- Group discussion allows teachers to get to know their students better. Although teachers want to treat their students as individuals, few teachers get to know their students well. Working with each student individually seems like a logical answer, but it is not often possible, and even when it is possible, students are sometimes more likely to reveal their true attitudes and feelings when sharing them with peers. When students become involved in group discussion, students and teacher begin to know one another in ways that would otherwise be closed.

11
chapter

Self Encouragement

Teaching can be frustrating, discouraging business. Teachers and parents (for parents are also engaged in teaching) seldom live up to their own or others' expectations. At one time or another, we feel unappreciated, exhausted, resentful, angry, impatient, upset, frustrated, betrayed, sick, and discouraged. What makes these feelings worse is that they're often a secret. Good teachers aren't supposed to have these feelings. Good teachers aren't supposed to have problems, either.

Teachers are encouraged by their teacher-education professors, by the role model that is held up to them by society, and by their aspirations to become super-teachers—teachers who help every child, who solve every problem, who meet every need. Many new teachers find themselves feeling much like an experienced teacher who described her early view of herself: "I thought of myself as God's gift to the teaching profession."

Giving Up the Super-Teacher Ideal. One reason this chapter is last is that its main point can be understood only in the context of the rest of the book. The purpose of this book is to help teachers be more effective; the purpose of this chapter is to persuade teachers to give up the idea of becoming or even wanting to become super-teachers. A super-teacher is more kind, patient, knowledgeable, understanding, cheerful, stimulating and helpful than ordinary mortals. Each of us has an idea of what a super-teacher is, and it is this idea that you may take as your definition. The ideal of striving to become a super-teacher is meant to encourage teachers to do a better job, but its actual effect is to discourage them.

Trying to be perfect can get in the way of accomplishing things. Dreikurs liked to talk about the "courage to imperfect" (Dreikurs, 1971, p. 10). Many things remain untried or undone because we are not willing to fail, to make mistakes, to be imperfect.

Many different psychological theories talk about perfectionistic ideas and how they lead to self-defeating behavior. Adlerians (Adler, 1970; Ansbacher and Ansbacher, 1956, Dreikurs, 1971) talk about mistaken ideas, Ellis (1957, 1975, 1977, 1978) talks about irrational ideas, transactional analysis (Berne, 1976, Steiner, 1974) talks about life script and beliefs that contribute to a life script. All of these theories concern themselves with self-defeating, discouraging results that come of unrealistic, perfectionistic expectations. In *Teacher Effectiveness Training* (T.E.T.), Gordon (1974) applies these concerns to teaching and calls such expectations "myths." An exercise I have used to help teachers become aware of their own myths about teaching is to make a list of their own myths after having read Gordon's discussion in T.E.T. Here is one such list:

- To be a good and fair teacher, you must be consistent in the way you treat your students.

- A good teacher must never show favoritism.
- I must do everything perfectly.
- There is a certain activity that each individual does better than anyone else.
- Put the people I am close to first and myself second.
- A good teacher supports the other teachers and administrators even though he or she does not believe in what they are doing.
- All students will be attentive and cooperative and will want to learn if you employ methods of teaching that encourage student participation.

What makes these statements myths is the idea that they are necessarily true, that good teachers necessarily fit this description all the time, and that you are not a good teacher if you don't fit this description all the time. What makes such statements irrational is, as Ellis likes to point out (1961; 1962), that they confuse what may be desirable with what *must* be, what *has* to be.

When we tell ourselves that things *have to be* a certain way, we set ourselves up to be frustrated. Frustration leads to discouragement, and discouragement results in less effective teaching.

Why the Myths Don't Work. Attempting to live up to perfectionistic expectations of being a super-teacher doesn't work because such expectations are concerned with self-image rather than with being effective. Teachers who try to live up to their own or others' expectations are constantly looking over their own shoulders to see how they're doing. They're constantly comparing how they're doing with how they would like to be doing and then feeling good if things have gone as they expected and feeling bad if things have not gone as expected. The myths may motivate us to try harder in individual instances, but in the long run, they lead to discouragement when we can't meet expectations.

Whereas living up to perfectionistic myths encourages concern for self-image, the courage to be imperfect comes from a concern for something outside ourselves. As a teacher, I've found that concern about "how I'm doing" or concern about how others think I'm doing creates anxiety and is de-energizing. On the other hand, being concerned with completing a job, listening to a student, solving a problem, or doing anything that is more important at that moment than I am — more important than my self-image — is usually interesting and encouraging even when I can't accomplish what I would like to do.

Concern about how we're doing is understandable. Teaching is a profession that puts the individual in the position of being almost continually judged by other people—students, other teachers, parents, administrators, and members of the community. Outside of being an entertainer, few professionals have so many "publics" that they are expected to please. Being expected to please all of these groups encourages a preoccupation with "how am I doing," but this very concern encourages us to focus on the wrong thing — ourselves.

ALTERNATIVES TO
TEACHER MYTHS

Teachers often have the same fear of failure that their students have. This fear of failure is often related to the high standards — often, impossible standards — that society sets for teachers. As students have more and more difficulties, the school and the community put more and more pressure on teachers. Teachers cannot always change the beliefs of others, but they can change their own beliefs about what is realistic. Here are some of the substitutes for the myth of the good teacher that I have found helpful in my own teaching:

- I am in the class to meet my own needs as well as the student's needs. As long as I am not using students or other people to meet my own needs, I have a perfect right to meet my needs.

- I will be more flexible, creative, and effective if I avoid constantly asking myself, "How did it go? Was I successful or not? Did I do a good job?" Constant evaluation can easily become an ego trip: I feel good if I feel I did a good job; I feel badly if things don't go as I expected.

- I cannot succeed with every student. There are some students who are not ready to change; there are some students who need what I can't give them. Getting mad at myself or at them will not help me or them. This attitude, far from being defeatist, allows me to continue working with students with whom I am not succeeding without discouraging them further.

- Feeling guilty will not make me effective or happy. Feeling guilty only discourages me. If I am unhappy with what I'm doing or not doing, I am better off to think of what I can do about it.

- I have a right to make mistakes and to admit that I have done so without apologizing, feeling guilty, or putting myself down.

- When I feel discouraged, I'm usually avoiding something. If I can find out what I'm avoiding and then tackle that thing head on, my discouragement usually disappears.

- No one has the right to make unlimited demands on me. When I don't decide what I'm willing to do and what I'm not willing to do, I end up feeling used.

- Unlimited devotion is not a virtue. I need to insist on time for myself, when I don't allow my work or other people to make demands on me. This area of jealously, selfishly guarded time and space encourages and renews me.

- I am appreciated more by others and I respect myself more when I don't automatically say "yes" when others ask me to do things. When I *do* agree to do something, I feel that I do a better job and am more cooperative because I know that I could have said no.

- I have the right to accept responsibility for my own behavior. I would like to please everyone, but I know that I can't. This being the case, I can listen to others' opinions, but I need to remain the final judge of what I will do or not do.

MUTUAL SUPPORT

Supportive colleagues are essential. Each time I have worked with a group of teachers, I have noticed that what is most encouraging to the people in the class is the other people in the class. The encouragement they feel seems to come from a number of experiences:

- The realization that "I'm not alone." People feel more sane, less defensive, and less isolated once they realize that everyone has the same problems.
- The experience of acceptance. When people accept one another without judging, they help one another grow.
- Finding listeners. When people begin to listen to one another, they feel understood and accepted, even when they do not agree with one another.

Each semester, as I begin my graduate class for teachers, I make the point that the class is designed to help the individuals in the class with specific problems and that this can happen only if class members share problems, listen, and encourage one another. At first, no one wants to admit to having problems. Everyone feels that his or her problems and inadequacies are a secret. After trust begins to develop, people begin to find that the only secret is that everyone else has problems and frustrations, too. The realization that everyone has problems is one of the most beneficial aspects of the class. The real discouragement in teaching comes not from making mistakes or doing things badly, but rather from having to pretend that there are no problems.

ACCEPTING RESPONSIBILITY

If anything, most teachers I have met are inclined to accept too much responsibility — especially for other people. Often, however, there are several areas where accepting responsibility can be encouraging.

Responsibility for Feelings. Accepting responsibility for my feelings means accepting that other people cannot make me feel the way I do unless I agree. I cooperate with others by feeling the way they want me to.

By accepting responsibility for my feelings, I can begin to work at changing those feelings.

Changing feelings is not easy, but accepting responsibility for them is the first step. We often feel the way we do because of what we tell ourselves (Ellis, 1977). By changing what we tell ourselves, we can change how we feel. For example, over the years I have heard teachers complain about a principal or other administrator who successfully intimidated most of the teachers. After much discussion, the teacher involved would begin to realize that he or she allowed him- or herself to be intimidated by the principal's behavior and that the principal probably wouldn't know what to do if the teacher refused to be intimidated.

Changing my feelings may be difficult, but it is worth working on, particularly when others use feelings as a way to manipulate me. Although accepting responsibility for others' behavior is often discouraging and draining, accepting responsibility for one's own behavior, even when it leads to hard work, is encouraging because it leads to the following realization: I have power over what I do, over what happens to me, and over how I feel. I can change.

Responsibility for Behavior. Many teachers desperately need to experience being self-directing. They feel caught in the middle between students on one side and parents, administrators, and the community on the other.

The discussions in previous chapters on power struggles, on responsibility, on the fear of failure, and on encouragement all focus on enabling students to feel that they have power over their own actions and that they have the power to change themselves and what happens to them. Teachers also need to feel that they have control over what they do and over what happens to them. The first step in assuming control over one's own behavior is to accept responsibility for that behavior.

There are some administrators, parents, and school board members who do not want teachers to experience control over what they do. Teachers who feel in control of their own behavior pose a threat because they are less willing to be manipulated, less pliable, and less docile. What we need to realize, however, is that no one can prevent teachers from having that control. We already have control over what we do, and no one can take that away. What we haven't done, in many instances, is to accept responsibility for the fact that we do choose, that we do decide, and that we do control our actions. When we don't accept responsibility for our actions, we end up feeling controlled.

Teachers can feel that they do have control over what they do only if they are willing to give up trying to control others—for example, students. Rather than this making them less effective, they are more likely to act effectively. They can no longer be easily drawn into power struggles, and they can no longer be easily defeated, because they refuse to put themselves in a win-or-lose position.

Of course, the teacher who does accept responsibility for his or her own feelings and behavior will still make mistakes, will still get into power struggles (though not as frequently), and will still find that there are students he or she doesn't know what to do with. Even these situations, however, don't need to result in discouragement if a teacher is able to accept responsibility without blaming him- or herself or feeling guilty and then to think about what's to be done.

Accepting responsibility is encouraging, not because it solves all problems but because it gives us a mechanism for coping with problems—those that can be solved and those that can't. There are no super-teachers in the real world who can avoid or solve all problems; there *are* teachers who accept responsibility for what they feel and do.

Accepting Conditions as They Are. Accepting things as they are means not wasting time being upset, shocked, frustrated, or angry that things are the way they are. Accepting things as they are is encouraging because it allows us to concentrate on coping with real situations. Some people feel that things will never change if they accept them the way they are. The opposite is the case. It is easy to spend our time and energy talking about the way things *should* be and to be upset that they aren't different, but this is self-defeating. We put our energy into complaining instead of taking action.

One day on a radio program on the schools, I heard a teacher talk about how tragic it was that children were not as they once were and that they expected teachers to be entertainers. He complained that the student had the nerve to tell the teacher that it was the teacher's job to remind the student and to make sure he or she did his or her work. The teacher sounded upset and shocked that students are this way, and he seemed to take the student's request for unnecessary service as a personal affront. The teacher was describing an unfortunate situation that every teacher faces, so we might as well accept it as a fact of life and start coping with it. It is futile to talk about the way things were or the way they should be. Neither helps teachers to deal with everyday situations.

As soon as we tell ourselves that life *should* be different than it is or that people *should* act differently, we easily start feeling sorry for ourselves and start discouraging ourselves.

Accepting Self. Accepting oneself means not wasting time worrying, blaming, or feeling guilty about what you *should have* done. Accepting oneself is encouraging because it allows us to concentrate on what we could do differently. We can't easily change the way we *are,* but we *can* change what we do.

Guilt, worry, and self-blame are ways of keeping ourselves busy without accomplishing anything. When I find myself worrying, feeling guilty, blaming myself, or feeling sorry for myself, I'm usually avoiding doing something.

Accepting Responsibility for Discouragement. Feeling discouraged is something we do to ourselves. Feeling discouraged lets us retreat or withdraw from a situation without accepting responsibility. For example, when we can't live up to our own or others' expectations, we can avoid doing anything by feeling discouraged. Feeling discouraged can be a way of avoiding something we want to avoid but don't want to make a decision about. By becoming discouraged, however, we undermine our self-confidence and our sense of directing our own lives. If you don't want to do something, make a decision: "I don't want to do this, and I'm not going to do it" or "I don't want to do this but I'll do it anyway."

Sometimes, we avoid a task by feeling discouraged and by telling ourselves, "What's the use? It doesn't make any difference anyway. It's not that good." And so on. When we try to force ourselves to live up to the expectations of others and then fail, we feel discouraged. The only way to avoid this discouragement is by giving up trying to be perfect, trying to be super-teachers, and trying to meet everyone's expectations. Some people have told me that this approach is defeatist. They feel that they have to have a goal they're constantly trying to reach, that they have to have something to strive for. What they don't realize is that they would be more likely to achieve their goals if they gave up their perfectionistic expectations.

One reason we find ourselves becoming discouraged is that we have been manipulated and trained into thinking too much about how we're doing and about what other people will think. This is seen by some as a cultural phenomenon. In *The Culture of Narcissism*, Christopher Lasch (1978) points out that a loss of confidence — a loss of courage — is related to the emphasis on personal performance as opposed to a concern for the work itself. I think that we overemphasize the teacher's personality and the teacher's ability to motivate, to discipline, and so on, and underemphasize what the students are learning. Teachers are human beings, no worse and probably no better than any group of human beings. By accepting this fact, we are less likely to discourage ourselves for not being perfect and to concentrate instead on effective teaching.

SUMMARY

Working to achieve a sense of control over our own behavior and over what happens to us is the secret of self-encouragement. When we try to live up to the ideal of super-teacher, we inevitably find ourselves discouraged because we can't control other people — students, administrators, and parents. We can't control their expectations, what they think of us, or their behavior. By accepting responsibility for our own feelings and behavior, we feel encouraged because we can then begin to take charge of our lives. The more we concentrate on what we can do, the less helpless we feel. The more teachers encourage students to concentrate on what they can do, the less helpless students will feel. The less helpless and controlled teacher and students feel, the more responsible they are likely to be.

REFERENCES

Adler, A. *Superiority and social interest* (2nd ed.). H.L. Ansbacher & R.R. Ansbacher (Eds.). Evanston, Illinois: Northwestern University Press, 1970.

Ansbacher, H.L., & Ansbacher, R.R. (Eds.). *The individual psychology of Alfred Adler.* New York: Basic Books, 1956.

Bell, G.D. *Analysis of teacher behavior.* Unpublished manuscript, 1978.

Berne, E. *Beyond games and scripts.* New York: Grove Press, Inc., 1976.

Dreikurs, R. *Fundamentals of Adlerian psychology.* Chicago: Alfred Adler Institute of Chicago, 1953.

——. *The challenge of parenthood* (Rev. ed.). New York: Hawthorn Books, 1958.

——. *Psychodynamics, psychotherapy, and counseling: Collected papers of Rudolf Dreikurs, M.D.* Chicago: Alfred Adler Institute of Chicago, 1967.

——. *Logical consequences.* New York: Hawthorn Books, 1968.

——. *Psychology in the classroom: A manual for teachers.* New York: Harper & Row, Pub., 1968.

——. *Social equality: The challenge of today.* Chicago: Henry Regnery, 1971.

Dreikurs, R., Grunwald, B. & Pepper, F. *Maintaining sanity in the classroom.* New York: Harper & Row, Pub. 1971.

Ellis, A. *How to live with a neurotic.* New York: Crown, 1957.

——. *Reason and emotion in psychotherapy.* Secaucus, N.J.: The Citadel Press, 1977.

——. *How to raise an emotionally healthy, happy child.* Hollywood, Cal.: Wilshire, 1978.

Ellis, A., & Harper, R.A. *A new guide to rational living.* California: Wilshire Book Company, 1975.

Glasser, W. *Reality therapy.* New York: Harper & Row, Pub., 1965.

——. *Schools without failure.* New York: Harper & Row, Pub., 1969.

Gordon, T. *T.E.T.: Teacher effectiveness training.* New York: D. McKay, 1974.

Holt, J. *How children fail.* New York: Dell, 1964.

Korzybski, A. *Science and sanity.* Lancaster, Pa.: Lancaster Press, 1933.

Lasch, C. *The culture of narcissism.* New York: W.W. Norton & Company, 1978.

Rogers, C.R. *Freedom to learn.* Columbus, Ohio: Chas. E. Merrill, 1969.

——. *On becoming a person: A therapist's view of psychiatry.* Boston: Houghton Mifflin, 1970.

Rowe, M.B. Wait-time and rewards as instructional variables, their influence on language, logic, and fate control: Part one — Wait-time. *Journal of Research in Science Teaching,* 1974, *11,* 81-94.

Simon, S., Howe, L., & Kirschenbaum H. *Values clarification* (Rev. ed.). New York: Hart, 1978.

Smith, M.J. *When I say no, I feel guilty.* New York: Bantam Books, 1975.

Steiner, C. *Scripts people live.* New York: Bantam Books, 1974.

Index